Living with the Dominator

A book about the Freedom Programme

Pat Craven

Illustrated by Jacky Fleming

Living with the Dominator
First published in 2008 by Freedom Publishing
© Pat Craven 2008

Pat Craven
Freedom Programme
PO Box 41
Knighton
LD7 9AF
Tel: 01547 520 228
Fax: 01547 529 223
Mobile: 07789871309
email: freedomprogramme@btinternet.com
www.freedomprogramme.co.uk

Printed and bound in Great Britian.

ISBN-13: 978-0-9558827-0-8
ISBN-10: 0-9558827-0-8

Layout and typesetting by Brad Waters www.bradwaters.com
Illustrations © Jacky Fleming www.jackyfleming.co.uk

CONTENTS

For more information about the
Freedom Programme visit the website:

www.freedomprogramme.co.uk

1
AN INTRODUCTION

I have decided to write this book for all the people who for whatever reason have not been able to attend a Freedom Programme, or the training, but have asked for more information about it. It is basically a summary of the information given in the handouts and some that I give verbally. The book is not to be used to facilitate the Freedom Programme, but to provide information to individual readers.

The other aspect of the programme that I cannot give you is the camaraderie, friendship and fun that we get from attending a programme with a group of other people. So if you are a woman and it is possible for you to do so, please be inspired by this book to seek out a Freedom Programme near you. They are all free and run by wonderful welcoming women at venues across the U.K. A list of venues is provided with this book and this is updated regularly on my web site.

If you are a man who would like to change your behaviour, you too are most welcome to attend a programme near you. You can check the list of venues or look for updates on my web site. The men's programmes that I endorse are also run in a welcoming, friendly atmosphere and the men who have graduated say they enjoyed the experience.

I will begin by offering a short history of the programme. Between 1986 and 1996 I worked as a Probation Officer. During that time I worked with hundreds of violent men. For some of that time I was a parole officer. Some of these men had committed murder and were released into the community under a provision known then as 'Life Licence'. Most of the murderers I met were men who had killed their female partners or former partners. I also acted as chairwoman to the management committee of the local women's Refuge and worked in the Refuge itself during that decade.

During those years I believed I had some understanding about domestic violence. I now know how wrong I was! In 1996 I went to work on the Probation Service Programme for male perpetrators of violence against women. For two years I sat with groups of men who had assaulted, raped and even killed women. I listened to these men and I began to realise several things. To my horror I recognised that I had unwittingly colluded with every abusive man I had ever met.

I also began to understand that no one else who worked in my field seemed to have the information that I was getting from working with these men. The third thing I learned was that there is a very common misapprehension that a woman who has been abused has some understanding of what has happened to her. This is simply not true. When a woman is being subjected to abuse she feels that she is in the middle of a very confusing mess and that it must be somehow her fault.

These revelations had a profound effect on me. It was like being possessed! I was a fifty-year-old supposedly experienced Probation Officer. I now realised that I had been living in a world of illusion. I became determined to get this information to other professionals and most of all, to all the women who are experiencing domestic abuse.

I ran my first Freedom Programme for women in 1999. It was basically a copy of the perpetrators' programme. I ran it for women who were on probation for committing offences that I could now see were a result of being subjected to abuse. I needed crèche facilities so I teamed up with a Social Services family centre and opened the programmes to any woman who wished to attend.

In 2002 I left the Probation Service to become a self-employed trainer. When I left I gave a sigh of relief at not having to work with abusive men any more. Wrong! Within weeks I received a request from a District Judge to provide a Freedom Programme for men. Soon I was back in the business of working with men.

I am writing this in 2007 and the men's programmes have been a great success. I judge that about sixty percent of the men who complete the programmes are changed. I also have reports from their female partners or former partners and from Social Workers and Health Professionals. The ideal situation is that the woman attends the Freedom Programme for women while the man is on the men's programme. If Social Services refer a man I will not accept him unless his partner has completed the Freedom Programme for women. I then invite her to observe the men's programme. This gives the women the knowledge they need to protect themselves and their children even if he does not change his behaviour. Recently two couples who have completed the programme have been reunited with their children.

During the last few years I have moved away from the concept of calling the men who attend my programmes 'perpetrators'. Instead I now present information to any man who is interested. I call them 'students' and give them a certificate of completion. This allows the programmes to be used in schools and to be part of a broader learning experience such as an open college network.

Initially I ran the men's programmes over twelve weeks. Some men did not complete the whole programme. This was often due to work commitments. Now I run them over two days, usually over a weekend. This has a visibly greater impact. I watch them changing. Most of them complete the whole programme. They are not allowed to discuss their personal circumstances. This means I do not waste time challenging victim blaming or minimisation. It also means that if a man is a genuine victim he can attend. Gay men can also feel comfortable. Male professionals such as Social Workers or Probation Officers can also join the men's weekend and use it as awareness raising training.

At the time of writing I provide training for facilitators and run weekend men's programmes. I also sell licenses to experienced facilitators so they too can train others to facilitate the programme. I am also in partnership with Certain Curtain Theatre Company and we put on conferences, which include performances of their wonderful play 'Lady in Red'.

All the information in this book comes from the thousands of men and women with whom I have worked since 1996.

2
THE DOMINATOR

In Britain 112 women a year are killed by a male partner or former partner. (Home Office 2007)

In Britain 22 men a year are killed by a female partner or former partner. (Home Office 2007)

The majority of women who kill their partners have been subjected to prolonged and severe violence.

From the available statistics it is clear that in the majority of cases the perpetrators of domestic abuse are men and the majority of victims are women. The next question to ask is, why do they do this? When we women are on the receiving end of violence and abuse we often ask ourselves this question. We also try to answer it.

Perpetrators tell us and we believe, that the violence was caused by drink, stress, unemployment, overwork, low self-esteem or insecurity. Many of the professionals we meet also accept these explanations. The reality is that these are all excuses. They may have been drunk when they hit us but they didn't usually hit anyone else. Being insecure doesn't make people violent. Why should it?

The real reason for their violence and abuse is the desire to keep women under control. They do not need to use violence every day. Some abusive men never need to use it at all, because they can control us by using other tactics. They will usually use violence when they believe the other tactics are failing.

Some women can also use many of the controlling and abusive tactics of the **Dominator**. The difference is that in the case of abusive men they are more likely to use violence when they believe the tactics of control are failing. As a result, a woman is murdered every three days.

Some of the tactics used to achieve power and control are depicted now in the analysis of the **Dominator**. In this chapter we will have a brief look at some of these tactics and will return later to examine them all in greater detail.

The Dominator was inspired by the Duluth Domestic Violence Intervention Project in Minnesota. He is one man but I describe him as changing into the other characters to use different kinds of controlling behaviour. He can change from one character to another with lightning speed. Often, when I show him to women on the programme they say, "You must have met my husband!" I joke that I believe that all abusive men are abducted when they are six months old and taken to a school in the mountains where they all learn to do and say exactly the same thing! One of the first people I trained to run the Freedom Programme was a specialist Domestic Violence Police Officer. When she started her programme her group was comprised of women whose abusers had been arrested and charged by her. She had also accompanied the women to court and knew their histories. One of the women looked at her picture of **the Dominator** and then compared it to everyone else's **Dominator**. She said that it was so like her partner that she initially believed each one had been done for an individual man from their police records and case histories.

The Bully
He uses **intimidation** to control his partner by: shouting, glaring, sulking, driving too fast and firing questions at her without giving her a chance to answer. As a result, she believes he is angry and tries to placate him. The men on my Programme have told me that **the Bully** is *not* angry. He is cool, calm and collected and completely in control of his emotions. What does he have to be angry about?

The Headworker
He uses **emotional abuse** to control his partner by telling her she is stupid, ugly, and incompetent. He is unfaithful and he puts her down in front of others, usually using humour. As a result she loses all self-confidence.

The Jailer
He **isolates** his partner by sulking when her friends visit. He refuses to look after the children when she has arranged to go out or go to work. He charms friends and family so they do not believe her. He moves her to remote places. As a result women are completely isolated.

THE DOMINATOR IS HIS NAME
CONTROLLING WOMEN IS HIS GAME

THE SEXUAL CONTROLLER
- Rapes you.
- Won't accept no for an answer.
- Keeps you pregnant OR
- Rejects your advances.

THE BULLY
- Glares.
- Shouts.
- Smashes things.
- Sulks.

KING OF THE CASTLE
- Treats you as a servant/slave.
- Says women are for sex, cooking and housework.
- Expects sex on demand.
- Controls all the money.

THE JAILER
- Stops you from working and seeing friends.
- Tells you what to wear.
- Keeps you in the house.
- Seduces your friends/family.

The Dominator

THE BADFATHER
- Says you are a bad mother.
- Turns the children against you.
- Uses access to harass you.
- Threatens to take the children away.
- Persuades you to have 'his' baby, and then refuses to help you care for it.

THE LIAR
- Denies any abuse.
- Says it was 'only' a slap.
- Blames drink, drugs, stress, over-work, you, unemployment etc.

THE PERSUADER
- Threatens to hurt or kill you or the children.
- Cries.
- Says he loves you.
- Threatens to kill himself.
- Threatens to report you to Social Services, DSS etc.

THE HEADWORKER
- Puts you down.
- Tells you you're too fat, too thin, ugly, stupid, useless etc.

11

The Liar

He makes the abuse seem *less* than it was by using the '*only*' word. For example, it was '*only* a slap'. When the 'only' word is used the listener does not really hear the rest of the sentence. He also *denies* there was any abuse or he *blames* the victim. Many men come to the programme asking me to help them to deal with this horrible woman who forces them to be violent. **The Liar** also uses a bewildering array of *excuses*. He blames drink, drugs, overwork and unemployment. He blames loss of temper, low self-esteem and insecurity. As a result his victim and many other professionals believe him.

The Badfather

He **uses the children** to control his partner. He turns them against their mother. If she leaves him he uses the courts to harass her for access. He denies paternity and tells her she is a bad mother. As a result women can have their children removed. He can seriously damage their ability to parent effectively.

The King of the Castle

He controls his partner by **treating her like a servant** and expecting her to do all the dirty, menial jobs. He controls the money and makes all the major decisions. As a result, women can come to believe they are second-class citizens. The men on the first programme I ran used to say that women are for 'CFCs'. Cooking, fucking and cleaning. Since then I have also heard 'WIFE'. Washing, ironing, fucking etc.

The Sexual Controller
He uses **sex** to control his partner. He refuses sex, demands sex, and rapes her. As a result women feel dirty and used and unable to stand up to him.

The Persuader
This persona comes into play if his partner has left the relationship or reported him to the police. He uses **coercion or threats** to persuade or frighten her into resuming the relationship. He wheedles his way back into the relationship by threatening suicide, crying and saying he has nowhere to go. He threatens to hurt the pets. As a result women have him back and drop charges.

These tactics can also be used in same sex relationships. Therefore the **Dominator** can be an abusive gay woman or an abusive gay man.

Why does the Dominator want to control women?
The behaviour of the Dominator is based upon his beliefs. This applies to everyone. All our actions are motivated by our beliefs. They are the engines which drive our behaviour. We often do not actually know what we believe. If we think about our beliefs at all we see them as facts. The Dominator holds hundreds of beliefs which allow him to abuse us. Many of them contradict each other. This is known as '*cognitive dissonance*'.

The Dominator gets these beliefs from whichever society he lives in. He is not a deviant but a product of his society. He is universal as all abusive men share his beliefs and use his tactics. The origins of his beliefs and the social reinforcements may differ between societies but his beliefs remain fundamentally the same.

In this book we will be mainly looking at the ways British culture and history have influenced the beliefs of **the Dominator** and all who live alongside him. However, if you come from a different culture you can use the same approach to make parallel observations about the ways in which your culture influences abusive men.

Women also live in the same society as **the Dominator**. We are therefore subject to the same conditioning. We may also hold many of the beliefs of the Dominator without being aware of it.

During the course of this book I will list the tactics and beliefs of each aspect of **the Dominator**. I will add which beliefs we women may share. I have gained this information from the hundreds of women survivors and male perpetrators I have worked with over the last nine years. Every anecdote I use comes from several men or women. I have not recounted any information, which comes from only one person.

We come to a very important point. Many women like men and want to have relationships with them. If we believe that all men are bastards we may stay with the one we have got. We may also hold the belief that the behaviour of the **Dominator** is normal. Many of us have sons and would like to help them to grow into non-abusive men. Therefore, before we continue with our exploration into **the Dominator** we will now meet a non-abusive man. **He is Mr. Right.**

NOT A SAINT THAT WE ARE SEEING
JUST A DECENT HUMAN BEING

THE LOVER
- Shows you physical affection without assuming it will lead to sex.
- Accepts your right to say no to sex.
- Shares responsibility for contraception etc.

THE FRIEND
- Talks to you.
- Listens to you.
- Is a companion.
- Has a sense of humour.
- Is cheerful.

THE PARTNER
- Does his share of the housework.
- Shares financial responsibility.
- Treats you as an equal.

THE LIBERATOR
- Welcomes your friends and family.
- Encourages you to have outside interests.
- Encourages you to develop your skills at work or at college..

The Friend

THE GOODFATHER
- Is a responsible parent.
- Is an equal parent.
- Supports your dealings with the children.

THE TRUTHTELLER
- Accepts responsibility.
- Admits to being wrong.

THE NEGOTIATOR
- Takes responsibility for his own well-being and happiness.
- Behaves like a reasonable human being.

THE CONFIDENCE BOOSTER
- Says you look good.
- Values your opinions.
- Supports your ambitions.
- Says you are competent.
- Values you.

Mr. Right is an example of a non-abusive human being. However, the characteristics of **Mr. Right** could be attributed to either sex. **Mr. Right** is a blueprint for a reasonable friend or partner or parent.

In this book I devote a chapter to each aspect of **the Dominator**. I will finish each chapter with a study of the non – abusive counterpart of that character. I will present a picture of an aspect of **'Mr. Right'** who is a non - abusive man. For example, if I devote a chapter to **the 'Bully'**, I will finish with **'The Friend'**.

3
THE BULLY

*In Britain a woman is killed by a violent partner
every three days.* London Home Office (2007)

*The Russian Government estimates that 14000 women
were killed by their partners or relatives in 1999.* (Amnesty 2007)

Examples of Tactics Used by the Bully to Intimidate

The Bully is excellent at using body language to intimidate. He uses every inch of his body the achieve this. Starting from the head down, he will glare or stare. He can make himself red in the face. He may grind or grit his teeth. He may splutter and foam at the mouth. He has a particularly menacing smile in that he smiles with his mouth and glares with his eyes. He also sneers.

He breathes heavily. He huffs and puffs. He uses a particular tone of voice. This could be flat and cold or he could shout. He can sulk and terrify his partner because she does not know what he is thinking. He may whistle and hum.

He invades his partner's personal space to intimidate her. He can lean over her or approach her from behind. He may come close to her face and rant or glare. He folds his arms, swings or taps his foot, drums his fingers or cracks his knuckles. He clenches his fists and fires questions at her without giving her a chance to answer.

As if that is not enough he kicks the walls or furniture and selectively smashes things. These things are usually her prized personal possessions. He may sit in an aggressive manner often thrusting his crotch and can puff himself up to make himself look larger. He uses secret gestures, which only she will recognize as a threat because of her past experiences with him. For example, he may use facial tics and certain words, which she knows from past experience to be a threat. He often sends the children to bed (a clear warning of trouble to come.)

He paces up and down. He bangs doors and slams things down on surfaces. He points. He makes sudden gestures and looks as though he is going to hit her but stops just before making contact.

He drives too fast when his partner and the children are passengers. He cleans weapons, blocks exits and hurts pets. He goes out without saying when he will return or where he is going. Women are then left in fear not knowing how he will behave when he returns.

These tactics can also be used in same sex relationships. Therefore the **Dominator** can be an abusive gay woman or an abusive gay man.

It is important to emphasise that **the Bully** is making the effort to use a sophisticated array of tactics. He is thinking clearly and he is completely in control of his emotions. **He is not therefore, angry.**

What does the Bully believe which allows him to behave in this way?

It is worth reminding ourselves that **the Bully** sees his beliefs as facts of life. He has never questioned these beliefs. He believes that all the behaviours we have identified are not abusive but normal. He knows that it is OK to bully to get his own way. He *knows* that this behaviour is manly and that real men are tough. He *knows* that men who don't bully are either gay or wimps. **The Bully** also believes that bullying works.

He *knows* that we are chattels and are owned by men. He knows that women like to be treated like this and need to be kept in order. He *knows* women are like pets and need controlling and protecting. He believes that women and dogs need to be trained. **Our Bully** *knows* women are inferior and men are superior in every way. If questioned about this belief he will usually say that this is because men are physically stronger.

This is an interesting example of confused reasoning. If he was right and men are superior to women because they are physically stronger, then he must believe all men are superior to all women because they are indeed stronger. However if he believes this then he must also believe that all physically strong creatures are superior to all physically less strong creatures. If that were true then the most superior creature in the world would be an elephant or a whale. These creatures would rule the world. This is patently not the case. **Our Bully** is mixing up or conflating two different concepts. Physical strength is not the same thing as superiority.

The Bully *knows* that violence is acceptable if you have a good excuse. This means that violence is acceptable if someone does something you do not like. I have lost count of the times I have heard groups of abusive men say it would be OK to kill your wife if you found her in bed with someone else. I often remind them that in the UK it is legal to have an affair or leave your partner. It is not legal to murder your female partner.

Where does our Bully get his beliefs from and how are they reinforced by the society he happens to live in?

Where shall we start? How about his childhood? **Our Bully** may have learned by example. He may have seen his father bullying his mother, his brothers bullying his sisters. He may also have copied his father by having tantrums to get his own way. This tactic may have been successful. Women can learn early not to challenge and to opt for a 'quiet life'. This would have reinforced the belief that bullying works. However, this is not necessarily the case. Many abusive men have non-abusive fathers. Many non-abusive men have had very violent fathers. Beliefs can come from many other sources outside the family.

The Bully himself may have been bullied at school and learned from that experience at an early or late age that bullying is effective.

The Bully may be a football fan. In a recent world cup game one player head butted another. The next day the media was full of the question; "What did the other player do to cause this assault?" This implication that the victim was to blame strongly reinforces the **Bully's** belief that women make men hit them.

The beliefs of **the Bully** may be reinforced by societal norms e.g. 'The rule of thumb'. This phrase is said to come from a time when it was acceptable in common law for a man to beat his wife with a stick as long as it was no thicker than his thumb. Recently I was listening to 'Gardeners Question Time' and I heard this quoted:

"A wife a dog and a walnut tree,
the more you beat them the better they be!"

As I stated at the beginning of this chapter, in Britain a violent partner kills a woman every three days. (London Home Office 2007). The depressing thing for me is that since I started the Freedom Programme in 1999 those statistics have not changed. Historically, most men who kill their female partners have been convicted of manslaughter instead of murder and consequently receive very short sentences. Abusive men have been receiving the message that it is easier to kill your wife than to divorce her and you will probably get to keep the house.

Until recently the marriage ceremony instructed us to 'love, honour and obey'. Women are 'given away' to their husbands by their fathers.

There are other cultural acceptances of bullying and violence. For example, culture and practice in the armed forces imply that it is desirable to use bullying as an acceptable way of training soldiers. I was listening to a radio programme about army conscription. A man recounted that he was conscripted when he was just eighteen and had left home for the first time. He spent the night in his billet and in the morning he laid his polished kit out on his bed for inspection. The Sergeant looked at it, shouted abuse at him and then threw it all out of the window. That is an example of the use of intimidation, which is designed to break the spirit of the recruit so the subject will obey orders. **Our Bully** uses it to achieve the same effect on his female partner.

Many of us enjoy action movies where men use violence to get their own way and are treated like heroes because they do. Recently there has been a long- running soap opera where an abusive male character has been using all the tactics of **the Dominator** to control his female partner. The men on my programme tell me that when they watched this drama they saw the depiction of this man as an example of how a 'real man' should treat women.

Sports such as boxing and wrestling give credence to violent behaviour. It is also legal in Britain to use violence against our own children. We smack them. When he was very small **our Bully** may have learned the lesson that it is acceptable to use violence when someone does something another person, in this case an adult, disliked. He may have been smacked for being 'naughty'.

Some popular songs glorify violence to women. For example songs with titles like

'Slap the Bitch'. There are other songs with more insidious messages. 'Delilah' tells of a man who saw himself as driven to kill his female partner because she was having an affair. The tone of the song is full of self-pity and he absolutely blames the victim. I understand that this song is the unofficial anthem of the Welsh Rugby team and is sung with feeling by thousands of supporters on a regular basis. There is a very popular computer game where participants shoot prostitutes.

The Bully's belief that women are inferior is supported by religious institutions, which insist that women cannot act as priests. The message is that we are not good enough. We are also paid less than men, which further reinforces this belief.

The behaviour of our government reinforces the beliefs of **the Bully** every time MPs debate in the House of Commons. They shout, jeer and interrupt each other. Political commentators describe such encounters as giving the opponent a 'bloody nose'. This is a description more suited to a prizefight. Commentators describe football, rugby and cricket matches in terms which could be used to describe a military battle. I heard the term 'dug out' used about the area where football managers watch the game.

Many presenters of current affairs and news programmes browbeat and interrupt interviewees. Viewers of so called 'reality television' watch avidly as contestants bully and abuse each other. This gives a powerful message that abusive behaviour is not only normal but also desirable.

Which of the beliefs of the Bully do many women share?

Many women have identified that before they attended the programme they 'craved' a man who would behave abusively and avoided men who did not. They felt that Mr. Right was dull because he was 'too nice'. They have told me that they saw **the Bully** as a strong man who can take charge. Many women have recognized that they assumed that men are superior because they are physically stronger. They, like the Bully, were conflating physical strength with superiority. Women have also recognized that they too believe that bullying works.

one day you'll wake up and see him as he really is - where you saw an Adonis you'll see a selfish child, where you saw a prince you'll see a FROG...

For centuries women have been used as sexual currency. We have provided sex and services in exchange for shelter and food. Now in a very small part of the world, a few women have the right to independence and paid work. However, centuries of conditioning are still with us whether we are aware of it or not. Many of us still expect to be kept by men and indeed feel that to be single and independent is a mark of failure. We also feel that we need 'looking after'. There is a very fine line between 'protecting' and 'controlling'.

The Fairy Story

Once upon a time there was an unmarried princess who ruled her land wisely and well. She made the laws, collected the taxes and was loved by all her subjects.

One day, when she was sitting by her lake, a frog hopped out of the water. "Hello Princess" said the frog. I am not really a frog at all, he continued. I am in fact, a handsome prince. A wicked witch turned me into a frog. However, if you kiss me I will regain my handsome human form. I will then marry you.

You can have my children and care for them. I would like about eight. You can wash my clothes and cook my meals. You can keep the

23

palace clean and tidy. I will take over as ruler and enforce the laws. I will be King. I will collect the taxes and keep all the money. I will of course give you a generous allowance for household expenses."

Later that night, when the princess was dining on sautéed frogs' legs in a tarragon, cream and brandy sauce, she said to herself, "I don't fucking think so!"

There is a serious point to this story. Why do so many of us 'jump at' the frog's offer?

and they lived happily ever after.....

How are women affected by the tactics used by the Bully?

When we live with **a Bully** we are walking on eggshells. We can never relax properly, as we are always awaiting the next outburst. We constantly try to second-guess him and to avoid antagonising him. We dare not disagree and we cannot express opinions. We dare not leave and we lose our confidence and become timid.

When we walk down the street we look at the ground. We are afraid to go to sleep. We are completely controlled.

We may become bullies ourselves and victimise other women or our children. Women have told me that they have got involved with even worse Bullies to protect them from the last one. We defer to men, and apologise all the time.

We feel brave when using alcohol or drugs so become dependent. We are afraid to show affection to the children in case he takes it out on them. We believe he is angry so we try to placate him. As I stated earlier this is not the case. What reason would he have to be angry?

THE NON-ABUSIVE COUNTERPART TO THE BULLY IS THE FRIEND. HE CAN BE AN EXAMPLE TO US ALL.

THE FRIEND

This is how the Friend behaves

He smiles with his mouth and with his eyes. His eyes are warm and friendly and this is because he is thinking warm and friendly thoughts about us. He is cheerful and pleasant and has a sense of humour. His posture is relaxed and open. His voice is calm and pleasant.

He talks to us and to the children and even more importantly he listens. He will engage in discussion and reasoned argument. If he disagrees he will accept our right to hold a different opinion and will not have to win every argument.

He is a companion in that he enjoys shared outings or treats. He is consistent in that he remains more or less the same person. The same person goes out in the morning and comes back in the evening. When he comes into the house he calls out, "Hello. I'm home! How are you?" This is in contrast to the **Bully** who walks in, ignores everybody and turns on the TV.

The Friend likes women and enjoys our company. He believes we are equal and worthy of respect. He accepts that he can be wrong and can admit it. He dislikes bullies and believes no-one has the right to control another adult human being.

4
THE BADFATHER

Women are 3 times more likely to be injured when pregnant. (Refuge 2007)

The men I have worked with told me that they only use violence when their 'feet are under the table'. That means that when a woman is pregnant she is more vulnerable and more dependent so they believe they will get away with it. They have also told me that when they look at a pregnant woman they see a fat, ugly 'thing'. They do not see a woman with a baby inside her.

The Badfather uses children to control and abuse us. It should be noted that the Badfather is not necessarily the biological father of the children he is using to manipulate us.

He turns the children against us
He employs a variety of tactics to turn the children against us. He undermines our authority, by countermanding our instructions. For example if we tell them to go to bed he will tell them to stay up late.

If we want them to eat their meal he will tell them they "don't have to eat that shit!"

He also turns the children against us by putting us down in front of them. He will make jokes about us to them and call us names in front of them. He will encourage the children to abuse us verbally and physically. Many women have told me that their children genuinely believe that their mother's name is a variation on 'slag' or 'filth'; because that is the only name they have ever heard their father or our abuser use.

He will buy their affection with expensive gifts that he has ensured we cannot afford. He will often do this after we have separated and he is refusing to pay for their support.

He uses the children to make us stay with him.

How does he do this? For a start he threatens to hurt or kill them if we leave. We must take these threats seriously as we have seen consistent news reports of abusive men killing children to punish their partners for leaving them. He also simply refuses to let them leave with us. He keeps one child with him at all times. If we try to end the relationship he cries in front of them and tells them we are forcing him out. He tells us we are depriving the children of a father if we don't want him back.

He makes them watch us having sex then threatens to tell the authorities that **we** insisted on this if we try to leave. As we have identified already he has taught them to prefer him so they would not want to leave with us and would blame us if we tried to go.

He abuses one child and indulges the other. This means that if we leave one will not want to go with us, but if we stay the other is damaged. What a terrible choice!

He uses the children to emotionally abuse us

When our new baby arrives he will not let us pick it up and nurse or cuddle it. He forces us to ignore the baby and leave it alone when it cries. He prevents us from feeding or changing the baby. Women have told me they were locked out of the room where the baby was crying. **The Badfather** has told them that they are 'spoiling' the baby if they attend to its needs. We comply in order to protect the baby. We fear that if we do pay attention to the child it will incur his wrath and in so doing will endanger the child.

We are then blamed by childcare workers for failing to 'bond' with our child. As we are so controlled and confused we often do not realise that he has actually prevented us from caring for the baby. We agree with the 'professionals' and blame ourselves. He also tells us we are bad mothers.

When we have separated and he has been granted access he will use this to abuse us. He will fail to turn up to collect the children. They are left waiting with their coats on. We are then left to deal with their distress.

He denies paternity and insists we have a DNA test. He also uses the reverse procedure and insists that he is the father when he is not. He will insist on DNA testing in this instance also. He persuades or forces us to become pregnant then persuades or forces us to have an abortion.

Many women on the programme have been subjected to the following tactic. He is violent and consequently the children are placed on the Social Services Child Protection Register. We are told that the children will be adopted if we have him back. He then relentlessly persuades us to take him back and often convinces us that Social Services would prefer him to be in the house to act as a father. We agree, have him back and the children are adopted. This can wreck our life. This is one of the worst things that he can do to us and yet he has not had to raise his hand or break a law.

He uses the children to isolate us

The Badfather persuades us to have children then refuses to help care for them. He refuses to look after them so we cannot go out to work or to see friends. He uses the term 'babysitting' when referring to caring for his own children. If he does look after them he does it so badly we dare not leave them with him again so we do not go to work or out with friends. He also asks the children to check up on us. He keeps us constantly pregnant. As soon as each child reaches school age he either rapes us or persuades us to have another.

If he fails to turn up for access visits this means that we cannot make arrangements to work or see friends at these times.

He uses the children to intimidate us

After we have separated from him, he bullies or assaults us when he collects the children for access visits. He uses the courts to harass us over access and custody. He comes round late at night drunk and shouting that he wants to "see my fucking kids!" He will break windows or doors in this frenzy of supposedly fatherly zeal.

When we have left him he uses the children to send messages to us. He may pin threatening notes inside their nappies. He will ask the children to tell us he is 'thinking of us'. He will ask the children if we are seeing anyone else. He will suggest outings and holidays that will only take place if we come along too.

He shouts at the children to intimidate us, and bullies them to punish us. He uses stepchildren as scapegoats. He abuses the children and us by making us afraid to show them affection.

What does the Badfather believe which allows him to behave this way?

The Badfather believes that only he has rights and his rights matter. He believes that women and children have no rights.

He believes that men own women and children and women and children are accessories. The children are 'his children' not 'our children'. It doesn't matter how violent he has been he still has the right to see the children whenever he wants. He believes that violence doesn't affect them.

What goes on in a man's home is no-one else's business. The home is 'his home' even though his name is not on the rent book. He believes that the behaviour we have listed is not abusive but is normal.

He also believes that childcare is 'Woman's work' and 'Real Men' don't do childcare. Women should stay at home with the children. He also holds conflicting beliefs about our ability to care for children. Women cannot cope with or discipline children. It therefore follows that it is better for children to have him in the home even if he has been violent. He believes he is a good father even if he is violent to us. (*Cognitive dissonance again!*)

Where does our Badfather get his beliefs from and how are they reinforced?

Once again we could start with his childhood where he may have learned his beliefs by observing the behaviour of both parents. They may be reinforced by the fact that the courts will grant access even to the most violent of men. Several case histories illustrating this point can be found on the Women's Aid web site.

This man may indeed have been violent, even abusive, towards his wife, but does that necessarily make him a bad father...?

His belief that we cannot cope without a man has been reinforced by generations of political and media propaganda, which stigmatises lone parents, who are usually women. Phrases such as 'women get themselves pregnant' are used with apparent credulity. I have to ask, "How do we do that? With a Turkey Baster?" Political parties support traditional married two parent families. They apparently discount the effect of male abuse on thousands of women and children.

Lone fathers are viewed with universal admiration. "Isn't he marvellous?" we say. "He had to give up work and go on benefit to care for them." "They are such a credit to him!" I would not decry the excellent job done by many lone fathers but when did we last hear anyone say that about a lone mother?

There are campaigning Fathers' organisations. They put out the message that fathers are denied access unreasonably. They have high profile patrons and picket the homes of judges.

The belief that real men don't do childcare is supported by such public figures as John Prescott, formerly the Deputy Prime Minister. When Cheri Booth had the last baby and Tony Blair took paternity leave, I heard him on the radio saying, "You wouldn't catch me changing nappies!"

HOW WOMEN ARE AFFECTED BY
THE TACTICS OF THE BADFATHER

The effects of turning the children against us

This tactic has wide ranging effects. We are unable to discipline our children for two reasons. One is because he has trained them to disobey us. The second is because he has destroyed all our confidence in our own ability to act as assertive parents. We are then labelled a 'bad mother'. The children prefer him. We lose contact with our children because we have to flee and leave them behind. Our children also physically and emotionally abuse us.

The effects of using the children to make us stay in the relationship

We are forced to stay in an abusive and dangerous situation and we need to remember that a violent partner kills a woman every three days in Britain.

We feel there is no escape. We are unable to leave because he always keeps at least one child with him. We resume the relationship because the children persuade us to. They are taken into care because we keep on taking him back.

The effects of using the children to emotionally abuse us

We are unable to make decisions because he has destroyed all our confidence.

We are seen as mentally ill. We feel guilty or inadequate. We feel as though we are only useful for childcare. We lack the confidence to find work, training etc. We then have no money, so we offend or defraud the benefit agency. Because we believe we are letting the children down without a man in the home we go back to the abuser or get involved with another one.

The effects of using the children to isolate us

If we are perpetually pregnant we cannot get out of the house to work or go to college. This is because we have no-one else to care for them. So even if by some miracle we did develop the confidence to work we would still be unable to do so.

THE GOODFATHER

How does the Goodfather behave?

The Goodfather knows the children. He even knows their names! He knows their birthdays, what they like to eat and the names of their friends.

He does his share of childcare tasks. He changes nappies, gets up in the night, and feeds them. He does his share of minding them, and does it properly. If we leave them with him to go to work or visit friends, we will find them fed and cared for and safe when we get home. We can then leave them with him again without having to worry. When he is caring for them he never describes himself as 'baby-sitting' his own children! If we wish to go out together he will take his turn at booking the babysitter.

He treats the girls and boys with equal respect and affection. He reasons with them if there are problems. He plays with them and communicates with them. He encourages non-stereotypical toys. He encourages the children to bring their friends home and to socialise.

The Goodfather encourages success at school or other areas of their lives. He helps with homework. He is financially responsible. He knows the children and knows their likes and dislikes. He knows what they like to eat and who their friends are.

The Goodfather treats us with respect, affection and admiration in front of the children. He will insist that they do the same. He supports our decisions. For example if we say it is bedtime he will back us up. He shares financial responsibility and accepts paternity.

He is good-humoured, pleasant and is consistent. He is responsible for his own behaviour and admits to being wrong. He tells the truth. He is a good role model.

The Goodfather believes that women and children have rights and deserve respect. He knows that women are perfectly capable of looking after children.

He also knows that he should do his share. He believes that violence and abuse should never be used in relationships and believes that children have a right to live in a happy peaceful environment. He likes women. He likes children.

5

THE EFFECTS OF DOMESTIC VIOLENCE AND ABUSE ON CHILDREN

At least 750,000 children a year witness domestic violence. Nearly three quarters of children live in households where domestic violence occurs. (Department of Health 2003)

I originally wrote the sessions on the effects of abuse on children in conjunction with two workers from the NSPCC. They had a lot of experience in dealing with children who had been traumatised by being exposed to domestic violence, and their expertise was invaluable. I no longer use much of the rest of the original Probation programme as my material has evolved and changed following the input of so many men and women who have completed the programme. However this session remains virtually unchanged and is powerful and effective when used with both perpetrators and survivors of abuse. For the purposes of this book I have combined two sessions of the programme into one chapter.

In order to discuss the effects on children in a focussed way, I have created three metaphorical groups. The first grouping is comprised of an unborn child, a pregnant woman and a newborn child. The second category focuses on a six year old and the third on a teenager. We now ask about the needs of the first group.

What does an unborn child, a pregnant woman and a newborn baby need to survive and thrive?

Shall we start with the pregnant mother? When we are pregnant we need good nutritious food and a calm atmosphere. We need plenty of rest. We need to attend regular medical checks. At this stage the needs of our unborn child are inextricably involved with our needs.

When we are giving birth there is a consensus that natural childbirth is the safest and that breast milk provides the best nutritional start to the baby's life.

When our baby is born it needs cuddling and to be told it is loved.

Our baby will feel loved and safe right from the start. It also needs to be fed and kept clean and warm.

How are we and our unborn child affected by violence and abuse?

As we are living with a **Bully** who also uses physical violence we are unlikely to experience a calm atmosphere at any time. Instead we will be physically and emotionally stressed. We will probably be short on sleep and constantly subjected to intimidation. There is evidence that unborn babies can hear and that our stress is communicated to them. They may be born with colic as a result.

As we have identified, statistically we are at greater risk of violence when we are pregnant. If we are being assaulted we may miscarry. Our baby could be born dead or premature. If **the Dominator** has kicked us his kick may have damaged the baby. The baby could then be born with brain damage and suffer for example, from epilepsy or cerebral palsy.

As we are living with a **Jailer** he may prevent us from keeping our medical appointments. Our general health and that of the unborn child can be compromised. He has alienated our friends and family so we have no emotional or practical support. He will refuse to look after the other children when we need to rest. There is no one else to help, so we do not rest. He may also refuse to let us have money for decent nutritious food. Again our health and that of the baby may suffer. Our baby may be born premature and or underweight.

The tactics of the **Headworker** can result in us abusing drugs and alcohol. Our baby's kidneys may be damaged. If he has told us we are fat and disgusting every time we eat anything we may become anorexic and our baby will not be properly nourished.

When the time comes to give birth, the tactics of the **Sexual Controller** may affect us. He may insist upon us having a caesarean and may force us to demand one. The medical staff will probably be told this is our choice. **The Sexual Controller** will probably also forbid us to breastfeed. Both these tactics will impede our ability to bond with our baby and may hinder its development.

Sexual controllers cut or break stitches so they can have sex after we have given birth. This can slow the recovery process. Every time we pick up our new baby to cuddle it he shouts at us that we will 'spoil' the baby. We are locked out of the room and forbidden to change or feed it. We are forced to listen to the baby crying.

If we cannot cuddle our new baby it will not have that early message that it is loved and will not begin to develop the self-confidence it needs in later life.

What does a six year old need to survive or to thrive?

Our six year old needs love. It needs to be cuddled and kissed and to be told it is loved. It needs this to help it grow into an adult with some sense of its own worth. It needs this love from significant powerful adults in its life.

Extended family members provide an essential balance for our children. They can be a sympathetic ear or an umpire who has influence within the family.

The next thing our child needs is safety. It needs to be in a physically safe environment and it needs to be taught self-protective strategies.

Security is also an emotional requirement. Our child needs to know that its world is a safe, predictable place. We give it this security with routine. Our child needs to know when it is time for school or bed and to know where it lives.

In order to provide this kind of security our child needs the powerful adults in its life to be consistent. This will ensure that the rules are consistent. If something they do is acceptable today it must be acceptable tomorrow. If one of their actions is wrong today it must also be wrong tomorrow.

Our child learns how to behave from a very early age from role models. It is watching us from its pram and absorbing essential lessons with its rusks.

We need to spend time communicating with our children. This gives them the stimulus to develop. That is how they learn to speak and read and to sing and draw. This is how they learn to have fun. They need fun. They need a house where people laugh and smile and play. They also need toys both for fun and to learn. Studies show that if a child receives this stimulus in pre school years they do better than children who have been left in front of the television.

Our children need friends. We all need friends to learn social skills and also to make us feel liked. If we have friends they tell us they like us. We will be starting our lives believing that our parents love us and our friends like us. This will help us to like ourselves.

Our children need to be kept clean and tidy and physically warm. They need appropriate clothing.

Our children need education. In order to achieve this they need to go to school.

While at school they need to be comfortable and accepted in order to learn.

In order to do well at school they need to sleep at night. Sleep also provides them with the rest they need to grow and develop.

Children also need food. They need nutrition to grow and develop and they need to know when that food will come. In other words they need regular meals. They also use food to learn how to eat socially. They will spend much of their adult life eating in the company of others so this skill is important.

In order to maintain good health our children need medical check ups. They need to make regular visits to the dentist and the school nurse.

Finally, if they are to make any sense of the world they live in they need to be told the truth. They need honesty. How else are they to grow into honest human beings?

How is a six-year-old child affected by violence and abuse?

Many women on the programme have told me that they dare not show their children affection as to do so will attract the attention of **the Dominator**. So in order to protect their children they have to virtually ignore them. This will deprive the child of the affection it needs to learn to like itself.

We are not allowed to communicate with our children any more than we are allowed to show them any affection. We cannot play with them, talk to them or sing to them. They are often left in front of the television, so they do not get the stimulus they need. They may have a slow start academically and intellectually for this reason also.

The Jailer has alienated all extended family members and close friends. There is now no one for the child to turn to for help.

Children in households where there is violence are not safe. They are killed or injured either deliberately or caught up in the cross fire whilst trying to protect their mother.

The next need we discussed was security. **The Dominator** will make sure there are no routines and no predictability. The family may be forced to move around. This may because of a tactic of **the Jailer** or because we flee with the children to refuges. School and other routines are disrupted.

The next need is consistency. In this house there is **a Dominator** who will change into a **Badfather** and a **Headworker**. He changes the rules and his behaviour all the time and no one knows what is going to happen next. Our children are confused and their behaviour can become bizarre.

When there is a **Dominator** in the house the children have him as a role model. For example the **Bully** is a giant baby who gets his own way by having tantrums. Our children will observe that tantrums work. They may then go off to nursery school or school and have tantrums. They then may be labelled as disruptive. Their education will begin to suffer. They may be diagnosed as suffering with ADHD. They may be prescribed medication.

Similarly children do not have much fun in the house of **the Dominator**. No one does. Their toys get broken too. This often happens at Christmas before they get a chance to play with them.

Although our children need friends they will not be able to bring friends home. They may be too embarrassed or simply not allowed. Other parents may not want their children to go into a house where there is known to be violence. As a result they will not be asked back to other children's houses and they will not have friends. This can cause loneliness and a failure to acquire social skills. It will be another reason why our child will not feel liked and feel unable to like itself. This could be another reason why our child is not doing well at school.

Sleep is very important to a child's development. However, if they are lying awake in bed listening to the sounds of battle below they are not going to sleep well, if at all. Whilst lying terrified in the dark they may wet the bed. They may then be smacked for this. Sometimes we are so busy trying to stay out of the way of **the Dominator** that we may not be able to clean them and dress them properly. They may go to school smelling of urine. This will further increase their isolation. If they have no friends they may be bullied,

Sometimes lack of sleep will destroy our child's ability to concentrate in school. They may also be worried about what is going on at home. Sometimes we are too bruised to take them so they miss days. So at six years old the rest of our child's life will start to be affected.

We mentioned regular nutritious meals. Most violence occurs either in the bedroom or when food is served. He shouts and screams and throws plates around. Interestingly many of the men on the programme have told me that they don't throw the food high up the wall. They throw it 'woman height'. This is so we can clean it off quickly without having to stand on a chair or a ladder. Our children may come to associate food with tension and fear and develop eating disorders. They may be so tense that they cannot swallow or they may hoard food or overeat when they have it in case there is no more for a while. Women have identified that their toddlers also throw plates of food at the wall.

Often **the Jailer** does not allow his partner to visit the dentist or the school nurse so our children do not get their medical check ups.

Illnesses can be missed, often to the detriment of the child's health. Their dental health can suffer markedly.

Finally we are often unable to tell them the truth. If they ask "why is Daddy hitting you?" We are often forced to lie. We deny it completely or we give them the excuses he uses. "Mummy deserved it. Daddy didn't mean it." They may hear him saying "Why are you making me do this to you?" or "I'm only doing this because I love you!"

Examples of the Beliefs Children May Develop

At six years old they may start to develop the beliefs, which will shape the rest of their lives. They may believe that women are stupid and should be subservient. Men are the bosses and women have no rights. They could be starting to believe that violence is normal and that violence means love. They have learned that bullying works.

They will also have heard the excuses used by the **Bully**. They will hear that we could not tell them how much we love them. They had no friends or extended family to do this. This may have diminished their self-confidence.

They may also have had a poor start at school at the age of six. They could have been underachieving since then. As a result they may continue to truant. They are still afraid to leave their mother alone and they also may be truanting because they are unpopular or bullied.

When **the Dominator** is terrorising us we encourage our children to get out of the house for their own protection. They may go to their rooms or out on the street. On the streets they will probably meet all the other children who have been similarly tipped out. A gang may form which could soon start to abuse drugs or alcohol and break the law.

These teenagers could have absorbed many of the beliefs of **the Dominator**. They may believe that violence is acceptable. Both boys and girls may be using violence in all sorts of situations. News reports tell of violent 'laddettes' or girls who are using violence often when drunk. They may assault the father to protect the mother. This can lead to criminal convictions or imprisonment. They are hearing that violence is acceptable if you have a good excuse.

They will also have heard their mother being called a slag. That will destroy their respect for her even if they don't know what it means. They will therefore learn early that to be a woman is to be something unpleasant. Children of both sexes can absorb these beliefs.

> *One in five young men and one in ten young women think*
> *that abuse or violence is acceptable.*
> (Zero Tolerance Charitable Trust 1998)

The needs of the teenager

Their needs should have been met when they were six and continued to be met in the intervening years. This did not happen and the effects of domestic abuse on the teenager are now cumulative. Teenage years are always difficult even when there is no abuse in the home. Life for a teenager with **a Dominator** is even harder.

The effects of Domestic Abuse on a teenager

We have identified many ways in which our newborn babies and six year olds have been affected by being exposed to domestic violence and abuse. Ten years later everything will probably be much worse.

Children of both sexes can abuse their mother emotionally and physically.

They could have eating disorders due to poor self-image or too many mealtimes marred by violence. They could also be self-harming especially if they have been sexually abused. Many women on my programme have been sexually abused as children.

42

Girls could be unable to refuse sex with boys because their self-image is too poor for them to believe they have the right to say no. They may not have the confidence to insist on protection from disease or pregnancy.

Girls may underachieve because they believe they are stupid, worthless and only good for CFCs. (Cooking Fucking and Cleaning) Boys may have learned to abuse their girlfriends.

In the programme for women and the programme for men we finish the session by making a list of the ways in which a child's life has improved when the **Dominator** is no longer in the home. This means either the woman has left him, had him removed by injunction or that he has done the Freedom Programme and changed from (as one women put it) 'horrible' to 'lovely'.

These are the improvements that the men and women in the programme have listed in the last nine years.

Women will tell each other that these things take time, as often the children are initially more difficult to deal with as a result of the tactics of the **Badfather**.

HOME IMPROVEMENTS

Improvements for the pregnant mother, foetus and newborn baby. The Dominator is gone when the mother is six months pregnant.

These improvements were all listed by women on the Freedom Programme. This means they have access to support. In some cases their partners have also done the programme.

The baby has a greater chance of being born at all because no one is kicking it while it is in the womb. As mothers we can also attend medical appointments and receive antenatal care. The baby has a much greater chance of being born healthy and any health problems can be identified and treated.

We have access to nutritious food and this too will affect the health of the baby. If there is no **Dominator** to constantly tell us we are fat we will feel able to eat properly. We can sleep at night. Our extended family can return to the home to help us with household tasks and to care for any other children. We can put our feet up in the afternoon. There is a calm atmosphere and we will not be subjected to stress. This in turn will affect the baby who is less likely to be born with colic.

When the **Dominator** is gone we may be able to stop using substances such as drugs, nicotine and alcohol. This could reduce the likelihood of the baby being born with damaged kidneys.

We can choose to give birth naturally and this will improve both our health and our ability to bond with the baby. We will also be able to breastfeed if we choose. This could provide the baby with the nutrients it needs to begin to develop good health.

When the baby is born we can begin to show the love and affection, which will provide the child with self-confidence for the rest of its life. We will also have the freedom and time to provide practical care for the baby. We will now be free to get up in the night to feed and clean it when it cries.

If the father has done the Freedom Programme he is much more likely to do his share of childcare so he will also get up in the night etc.

Improvements for a six year old.
The Dominator has gone when the child is five.
When the **Dominator** has gone we can show our children affection. We can tell them we love them and that they are loveable. They can sleep at night. This will make them livelier and more receptive to new experiences. This will lay the foundations for a successful school career. They may also stop wetting the bed. Until they do stop we are free to comfort them and clean them up to send them to school.

In the year before they go to school we are able to spend time with them and provide the stimulation they need. We can play, sing or read with them.

This will mean that when they get to school they will be much better able to adapt to the learning process.

Our friends and family are now welcome in the house. Our child has the chance to get to know relatives and to benefit from their support. So do we.

They can attend school and concentrate while they are there. Success at school will encourage them to try harder. They can invite friends into the house and begin to learn social skills. Their friends will tell them they like them so they will begin to like themselves. Having friends will also make their school lives happier and this will also encourage success. Extended family can now return to the house and give them that extra affection and support.

Meal times are now a pleasant experience. They are no longer terrified and forced to eat food they hate. Their relationship with food will improve and they may avoid future eating disorders. We are now free to tell them the truth and to answer their questions honestly. This will help them to begin to make more sense of the world. They can now attend medical appointments so their general health can improve.

We can communicate with them and now if they ask,"Why did Daddy hit you?" we can tell them the truth. We can say, "Daddy hit me because I did something he did not like and he was wrong to do this." This will start to counteract his or her belief that it is OK to use violence if someone does something you do not like. If their father has done the Freedom Programme he can also tell them this, which makes that message even more effective.

Improvements for teenagers.
The Dominator has gone when the child is thirteen.

Many of the improvements for the six year old will apply to the teenager. Their lives may be slower to improve but at least we will be allowed to help them cope with the past. We will now be able to listen to them and the Freedom Programme will help us to have a clearer understanding of their difficulties. We can also help them to approach other agencies for specialist counselling. We will no longer be prevented from telling other people about the situation. We can tell them the truth. We will be able to live more independent, happier lives and this in itself will have a positive effect on our teenage children. If their father has done the Freedom Programme he will make more of an effort to communicate with them and to help them understand his behaviour. He will be a vastly improved role model.

6

THE HEADWORKER

*It is estimated that one in four women will experience
domestic violence at some time in their lives.* (Home Office 2007)

My experience indicates that the true figure is far higher. If you ask
a woman if she has experienced domestic violence she will probably
answer no. Even if she is being hit she may not recognize this as
domestic violence. For example in my lifetime three different men
have actually hit me. It was only when I wrote and began to run
the Freedom Programme that I realized that I too have experienced
Domestic Violence.

The Headworker uses emotional abuse
He makes us feel stupid and useless and worthless
The Headworker is fond of using humour to achieve this. He likes
to make jokes about us in front of others. He jokes about our driving,
technical abilities etc.

When we speak he says "what!" then does the same when we repeat
what we said. He also repeats the last thing we said in a derogatory
tone. He corrects our use of language or the content of our remarks.

He tells us we are useless. Again, this often starts with humour. If we object he says "Can't you take a joke?"

He does not use our name. He calls us 'babe' or 'princess' or 'she' or 'the wife'. He also calls us other insulting names such as 'Slag', 'Bitch', 'Cow' and 'Whore'.

He may have an insulting pet name. He may call us, 'little pig' but insists it is a term of endearment. I am not saying that every man who does not use his partner's name is abusive, but I do know that every abusive man I have ever met does not call his partner by name.

He makes us feel ugly

He tells us we are too fat, thin, tall, small, old etc. Our tits are too big or too small and they sag. He tells us we are fat and ugly. This is very common when we are pregnant. He tells us all this constantly.

He tells us our vaginas are too big to give him sexual pleasure. This is a very commonly used tactic. Sometimes he tells us this is because of childbirth and we believe him until we come on the Freedom Programme and hear women who have never had children say the same thing. Midwives tell me this is a myth.

He compares us to other women on the TV. Singers and celebrities are favoured. This of course happens night after night because many people watch TV regularly. He is also unfaithful, often with our friend or sister.

He makes us think we are going mad

He moves or hides things and then denies it. He tells us something and then denies having said it. He tries to confuse us by moving goal posts and changing rules. The kettle should always be full or empty or half full, but this rule changes all the time. He tells us we must be suffering from PMS. He tells us we call out the name of former lovers in our sleep. We are then afraid to sleep.

He sets us up with other agencies so we will be diagnosed as mentally ill. I have heard variations on this story more than once. The abuser says to his wife "Quick! Call the police there are burglars in the attic!" She does so and when the police come he asks them who called them and apologises on her behalf. "Sorry she is always doing things like this." Soon she is known to local agencies and it is easier for to him to get custody of the children and get her out of the house.

He encourages us to visit the doctor and take tranquilisers. He encourages us to drink. When we are befuddled we are even easier to confuse. He then says, "I had to hit you because you are mad, drunk, or drugged."

What does the Headworker believe which allows him to behave in this way?

The Headworker believes we are so stupid that if he tells us something often enough we will believe him. He also believes that his behaviour is not abusive. He believes it is normal. He also believes that he has a right to use whatever means are at his disposal to control his partner. We should be subservient.

He believes that we are too feeble minded and incompetent to survive on our own, and we need men to look after us. He knows we are too feeble minded and incompetent to do work which requires intelligence or ability. He also knows that if women are successful in business it is because they slept their way to the top or are not 'real women'.

The Headworker does not like women. He believes we exist to be used by men.

He believes that women are dirty, we are slags, and we are pieces of meat and men own us. We are snakes with tits. We are snails with tits.

A woman friend of mine was parking her sports car when a small boy aged six or so called out, "That car is too good for a woman!" I heard a man in a pub telling his friends, " If you tell a woman she is stupid often enough she will soon believe it!" A taxi driver told me that all the other taxi drivers, the 'lads', were changing the voice settings on their satellite navigation systems to men's voices as they did not like being told where to go by a woman.

The Headworker hates the colour pink! Yes he really does. It reminds him of women. I was listening to the business news a couple of years ago on Radio 4. The reporter was describing how a German based concrete company had reported a large drop in profits in the UK. He said it was because they had changed the colour to pink and British builders could not bring themselves to use it.

Where does the Headworker get his beliefs from and how are they reinforced by whichever society he happens to live in?

Shall we start by considering where he gets his beliefs about our intelligence and abilities? He could have watched his father treating his mother with contempt. He could have been encouraged by his father to join in with this abusive behaviour.

There are hundreds of sexist jokes, both subtle and overt. For example there are jokes about women drivers. They are all derogatory. For example, "What do you get if you cut off a woman's legs?" Answer. "Snail trails."

When I was younger I used to go to Rugby clubs. I joined in dozens of songs, which were extremely abusive to women. At the time I did not notice this and sang along with gusto.

All the abusive men I have met believe that women can't drive. They insist on this even though insurance companies offer us cheaper premiums. If challenged they will insist that women actually cause accidents because we drive too slowly. The word 'Woman' is used as an insult from one man to another. So is the word 'Girl'.

Words like 'Bimbo' and 'Essex girl' and 'Airhead' all support the **Headworker's** view that we lack competence and ability. In recent years the Labour Party created one hundred new women MPs to redress the gender imbalance in Parliament. These highly qualified, intelligent and competent women are frequently referred to in the media as 'Blair's Babes'. This is patronising and insulting as it implies that they are not adult women and were only in Parliament on Tony Blair's sufferance.

The Headworker's beliefs are further supported by the fact that we are still paid less than men for doing the same job. Subtler messages are contained in advertisements. I recently heard a radio commercial for a car. The woman praised the car and then said words to the effect, "I will go home, slip into a little black number and get my John to give me one!" The implication is that we women are parasites who provide sex to our husbands in exchange for goods.

Let us examine **the Headworker's** belief that women are pieces of meat and have no other value. A popular joke amongst abusive men is this: "How can you trust something that bleeds for a week and doesn't die?" The view that we are pieces of meat is supported by several words and phrases in common use. A woman who is considered to be dressing too youthfully for her age is described as 'mutton dressed as lamb' or 'done up like a dog's dinner'. Pubs and clubs where men meet women are described as 'cattle markets' or 'meat markets'.

The expression 'spit roast' is used to describe a woman being penetrated by two men at the same time. Abusive men describe the sexual act as 'porking' and their penises as 'pork swords' or 'beef bayonets'. The lips to the vagina are described as 'beef curtains'. Women in my own home area of Merseyside are described as 'birds'.

Everywhere I go in the UK there is a local phrase, which is used to insult the size of a woman's vagina. In Merseyside we are compared to the 'Mersey Tunnel' and in Newcastle it was 'like a sausage up the Mile End Road'. I remember running the **Headworker** session with a large group of women. One by one they all said that their **Dominator** had told them that they had these huge sloppy vaginas. Then someone said, "Perhaps it is because he has such a small prick?"

At this point we all started to laugh, which was a very good thing because prior to this session many of us felt we were deformed. No one had ever told anyone else about this tactic. Then someone asked, "Is that why women get these 'Designer Vaginas'?" At this point I said that if I were contemplating such a purchase I would want a catalogue, with illustrations and titles like, 'The Litchfield' or 'The Balmoral'. Someone else then chipped in that if they had one they would want to show it off to friends. We then imagined a stick with a mirror on the end, which we could use for comparisons if we met our friends in the supermarket. By this time we were all helpless with laughter, but completely free of the delusion that there was anything wrong with any of us.

Shall we now consider magazines? Shall we go together into a news agency and look at the magazines for young people? Let us begin with the magazines for young teenage boys. Here we have a magazine for every conceivable hobby and sport. We have motorcycle magazines, music magazines, football magazines and computer magazines. Our boy will draw his pension before he reads them all.

Shall we now examine the magazines for teenage girls? When we do we will see that they are entirely devoted to the subject of how to be an attractive piece of meat. They print diets and advice on how to kiss or provide sex. They are virtually devoid of any information about careers or hobbies.

The beliefs we share
I have heard women say that other successful women must have slept their way to the top and many of us believe that men are better drivers (insurance companies don't.) We express surprise that women do successful jobs.

We sometimes assume successful, independent women are gay. A woman at a domestic violence prevention forum was heard to describe Freedom Programme facilitators as "a bunch of hairy legged lesbians." We call other women names like 'slag' and 'cow' and 'bitch'!

We believe men are cleverer and more skilful than us so when one moves into our home we lose our ability to do 'men's work' such as changing plugs.

How are women affected by living with a Headworker?
He is often very successful. We can feel hateful and ugly. Many thin women have come to the programme convinced they are grossly overweight. Many pregnant women come on the programme convinced they are grossly and disgustingly fat.

This can lead to eating disorders. We have plastic surgery, 'Designer Vaginas'. We have operations to enlarge our breasts. Someone recently told me that women are now having their anuses bleached and plucked.

Many women have been brainwashed into hating the women they have been compared to. Several women on the programme have overcome this by making themselves watch various singers. They start with a few minutes of a video or DVD and then increase the duration.

We may lack respect for all women, including ourselves. We can feel so bad about ourselves that we may abuse drugs or alcohol. If the **Headworker** convinces others and us that we are mad we may be diagnosed as mentally ill and given tranquilisers. Many women on the programme have been diagnosed as suffering from postnatal depression as a result of the tactics of the **Headworker**.

The Headworker makes us unable to trust our judgement or our decisions. This can lead to an inability to end abusive relationships or be an effective parent. He increases our dependence upon him and this can lead to unemployment or lack of confidence to train for work.

How are women affected by living in a society, which holds the beliefs of the Headworker?

We are never happy with ourselves. We are always on diets. We see other women as competition when we should be able to get support and help from one another.

We cannot achieve our full potential if we are constantly told we are stupid and useless.

The Nelson Mandela Story

If a person, or group of people are told often enough that they are inferior, they will probably come to accept that view, often without realising it. There is a parallel between sexism and racism. In South Africa, before independence, it was in the vested interest of white supremacists to belittle and exploit black people. It is in the interests of male supremacists to do the same to women. It is apparent that a similar 'brainwashing' technique has been used in both cases.

Several years ago I listened to a radio interview with Nelson Mandela. He was very aware of this cultural conditioning when he was leading Black South Africans to independence. He knew that his people had been told for years that they were stupid, inferior and incapable of governing themselves. They heard that they were not good enough to stay in the same room as a white person and they were certainly not good enough to be paid an equal wage.

Nelson Mandela was aware that at some level many black South Africans had absorbed these beliefs. He knew this because he recognised that even he had been affected by some of that collective inferiority complex.

In order to illustrate this, he talked of an experience he had when he had first been released from his long captivity on Robben Island. He said that when he approached the plane that was to fly him to freedom he noticed that the pilot was black. Just for a moment he caught himself wondering whether a black man could fly a plane. This story can be used to illustrate how our beliefs about ourselves can be influenced without our knowledge.

I would like us to consider how we would initially react if we were to board a plane and the pilot was a woman. Some of us would express pleasure and approval but that actually illustrates how rare it is to see a woman pilot. Many of us have admitted that we are more likely to say, "I hope she is not suffering from PMT!"

THE CONFIDENCE BOOSTER

This is how the Confidence Booster Behaves

He tells us we look good and enjoys our company. He values our opinions, abilities, talents and conversation. He talks to us and listens to us. He never makes abusive jokes about women and does not laugh when others do.

He supports our ambitions and encourages our endeavours. He encourages us to learn new skills.

He believes women are intelligent and worthy of respect. He also believes we are capable of doing any job we choose as well as a man.

He tells us that we are absolutely fine just the way we are!

7
THE JAILER

Every minute in the UK, the police receive a call from the public for assistance to deal with domestic violence. This leads to police receiving an estimated 1,300 calls each day or over 570,000 each year.
(Professor Stanko, E. 'The Day to Count: A Snapshot of the Impact of Domestic Violence in the UK'.
Criminal Justice 1:2, 2000.)

THE JAILER USES ISOLATION TO CONTROL US

He stops us from working or going to college
He refuses to care for the children or cares for them inadequately. For example he does not put them to bed and does not supervise them safely. He does not feed them and he telephones us so we can hear them crying in the background. This is an overlap with the **Badfather**.

He may also persuade us not to leave him alone or persuades us to stay in bed that day. We then call in sick and eventually lose our jobs. He says he wants us at home and says that he is jealous of our working with other men. He persuades us that he will look after us and that we don't need to work. He will say this even if he is unemployed.

He turns up at our place of work and is often drunk and abusive. He telephones all the time and is abusive to our colleagues and managers. He creates rows when we are trying to leave for work and alters clocks to make us late. He creates rows when we have to work late. He wipes our assignments off the computer.

He keeps us in the house

He prevents us from going out by actually locking us in the house. Some women I have met were locked in for years. He may paint the windows black so we do not know if it is day or night.

He goes out without taking his key. We then have wait in the house for him to return. He goes out and takes all the keys. He hides or destroys our clothes or shoes. He keeps us pregnant. He leaves impossible lists to keep us busy. He drives off with the buggy in the boot. Some **Jailers** have trained dogs to prevent women from moving from a certain place in the house.

He controls where we go and whom we see

He checks the mileage on the car. He demands bus tickets and train receipts. He calls us on the phone constantly. He buys us a videophone and demands that we show him where we are all the time. He times our visits to the supermarket and refuses to let us attend medical appointments for the children and ourselves.

He times us when we go out. He installs security cameras in every room so he can watch us all the time.

The Jailer stops us seeing our friends and family

When they call he may be wearing his underpants and watching TV. He will have the remote control in one hand and could be fiddling with his genitals with the other. The sound on the TV will be very loud and he will be watching either football or pornography. He will probably be wearing smelly socks and may also be farting, burping and spitting.

He will sulk when they visit. He will go and sit in another room and his disapproval will seep through the walls. Our friends ask, "Is he OK?" "Oh yes!" we reply. "He's just a bit shy." They will not want to linger or come back soon and we are so uncomfortable that we don't want them there.

The Jailer will also insult our friends and family when they visit. He may pick on us or start an argument in front of them. He may also seduce them, either sexually or by charming them so they do not believe us when we say he has been abusive. He may tell us our friends have tried to seduce him.

The Jailer tells us our friends don't really like us. He says they are using us and that they have made a pass at him. When we are getting ready to go out with our friends he may cause a row. He may say, "You are not going out in that are you?" He will proceed to tell us we look 'fat' or like a 'slag'!

The Jailer insists on having sex with us before we go out and will not let us wash.

He causes a row when we get home. He sniffs our knickers when we get home.

If we are having a night out he will turn up at the club or pub we have visited with our friends and then offers us a lift home.

The Jailer goes absolutely everywhere with us. We never see our friends alone. People think he is so devoted! He tells us that it is not safe for us to go out alone. He wants us to stay at home where he can 'protect' us.

The Jailer suggests that it would be very romantic to move somewhere in the country miles away from our friends and family. He may also persuade us that it is our duty to move to a distant part of the globe because he has a new job opportunity.

What does the Jailer believe which allows him to isolate us in this way?

The Jailer believes that a 'real man' keeps 'his woman' in the home. He *knows* that isolating women is normal, not abusive behaviour. Women are like pets and need to be kept in and controlled. Women cannot be trusted to go out alone.

The Jailer *knows* that women need to be controlled sexually and if we go out alone we will shag every man we see. He *knows* that all women are 'slags'.

He also *knows* that we are only really useful for CFCs and we cannot be trusted. He believes that men own women and that we are his property.

The Jailer also believes that women cannot do real work. Our wages are always 'pin money'. He will believe this even when we earn far more money than he does (Cognitive Dissonance again!). The Jailer *knows* that it is natural for women to be kept and that men are breadwinners. He will believe this even if he is unemployed and living off our wages. (More Cognitive Dissonance!).

Men on the Freedom Programme have been heard to say that the secret of a successful marriage is to, "keep her pregnant and hide her shoes."

Where does the Jailer get his beliefs from and how are they reinforced by the society in which he lives?

Once again we can start with **the Jailer's** childhood. Many of us will have grown up in families where women do not go out to work and they are not encouraged to have social lives.

There are many other social reinforcements. In the sporting world, sports such as football and cricket only receive publicity if played by men. When women play these sports the media largely ignores their achievements. This gives the message that our activities do not matter. Culturally we are not expected to take part in team activities.

I still can't believe this was the **ONLY** way to get women's football on TV...

There have been many sporting institutions such as cricket clubs or golf clubs which have refused to allow women to join. Workingmen's clubs, which refuse entry to women, also reinforce the message that we should not take our part in society.

After the last war a series of social policies were put in place to get women out of the workplace and into the home. We will see more of this when we get to the **King of the Castle**. One of these resulted in a situation where in the fifties women had to leave work when we married. Universities resisted admitting us for years and when they did we were not initially allowed to get degrees.

We were also traditionally prevented from taking an active part in society by laws which denied us the vote for so long.

The media also reinforces the beliefs of **the Jailer**. Movies and TV soaps have traditionally portrayed women as housebound. Current affairs programmes refer to us as *housewives*. There are countless television advertisements portraying women doing housework in a house.

The word 'housewife' itself implies that we should be indoors. There are other commonly used phrases such as 'her indoors'.

The belief that women need controlling sexually is reinforced by cultural practices across the globe. Genital mutilation is a prime example.

The beliefs we share

When we first meet **the Jailer** we interpret his isolationist tactics as a romantic desire to keep us to himself. We don't question his suggestions that we spend time with him and not our friends. Later we are grateful if we are 'allowed to go out' and we use phrases like, "He's really good, he '*lets*' me go out with my friends!" The use of the word 'let' illustrates that we believe he has a right to stop us. Some women criticize other women who do go out without their partners.

If we believe we need protecting we may be grateful if he wants to keep us safely at home.

HOW ARE WOMEN ARE AFFECTED BY LIVING WITH A JAILER?

If he has stopped us working or attending college we are affected in the following ways.

We leave our job or get the sack. We then lose our financial independence and have to rely on him or the state for money. We lose ambition and our self-esteem suffers as a consequence. We don't fulfil our potential by pursuing a career outside the home.

We drop out of college so we are unqualified and our earning threshold remains low. This again increases our dependence on him and makes it more difficult to leave him. We may look scruffy because we have no money to buy clothes.

Some women commit crimes because they have no money. When I was a probation officer, I met many women who had been arrested for shoplifting. They were stealing nappies and food. We have no money for buses taxis or other accommodation so it is difficult to actually leave him.

If he keeps us in the house we are affected in the following ways

Women in this situation are prisoners. I cannot believe how many women who have attended the Freedom Programme have literally been imprisoned in their homes. Those women are free to attend after they have left the relationship. We do not hear from the women who are still imprisoned.

When we are imprisoned we may become depressed or agoraphobic. We over-eat, starve, drink, or use drugs. We lose self-respect and strength of character and hate ourselves.

If he has cut us off from our friends and family we are affected in the following ways

One obvious and inevitable consequence is that we dump or lose our friends.

We have no one to tell about abuse so we have no support networks. We have no one to ask about the abuse so we do not get a second opinion. We are lonely and have no fun.

THE LIBERATOR

This is how the Liberator behaves

He encourages our friends and family to visit. When they do come he makes them welcome. He encourages us to go out with our friends. When we are all dressed up ready to go out with our friends he tells us we look great. He also says he will not wait up for us but will leave all the lights on to welcome us back.

The Liberator encourages us to work or study by bolstering our confidence. He provides practical assistance by cooking meals, doing his share of the housework and childcare. He encourages us to have our own interests and hobbies.

He trusts us and believes that women have the right to freedom. He believes that we can be successful at work in our own right. He believes we have a right to financial independence and that we can make a valuable contribution to the quality of our home situation.

8

THE SEXUAL CONTROLLER

*One in 20 women in England and Wales has been the
victim of rape. Only one in five attacks is reported to
the police. 'Current partners' (at the time of the attack)
were responsible for 45% of rapes reported to the
British Crime Survey. 'Strangers' were only
responsible for 8% of rapes.*
(Amnesty International 2007)

THE SEXUAL CONTROLLER USES SEX TO CONTROL US
HE MAKES US HAVE SEX WHEN WE DO NOT WANT TO

He uses persuasion
Women on the programme have described this as 'pester power'!
He wheedles and nags. He tells us it is our duty and if we don't want
sex then we don't love him. He tells us we are hurting his feelings
and makes us feel guilty. He tells us we must be frigid or a lesbian.
If we are expecting our family to visit he refuses to get dressed until
we have sex with him. He gets us drunk and gives us drugs. He tells
us sex is a medical necessity and without it his testicles will explode
all over the carpet. (In the Freedom Programme this is known as the
'exploding balls syndrome'!). He also tells us that without sex he will
get prostate cancer.

He uses bribery

He promises money for housekeeping or a new winter coat. The latter is a popular move in the autumn. He tells us that if he has more sex his behaviour will improve because he will not be so 'frustrated'.

He uses intimidation

He sulks. This is very powerful as it sends us the clear and simple message that unless we have sex he may use violence. Similarly he will stomp around slamming doors etc. We are then afraid that he will wake the children up so we give in. He also huffs and puffs and uses other tactics of intimidation. He doesn't actually have to say he will use other kinds of violence, but the threat is implicit.

What d'you mean
you don't fancy me
when I'm like this?
I'm like this
because I
HAVEN'T HAD
SEX !!!

The Sexual Controller intimidates us to make us have sex, when we don't want it, by shouting. Again we give in because we are afraid that others in the house, especially the children, will hear him.

He may also threaten to go elsewhere and these threats may concern the children. He may also accuse us of getting sex elsewhere if we do not want it with him. This is very intimidating as the next move could be to assault us on the pretext of jealousy.

Not only does the **Sexual Controller** bully us into having sex, but we also have to react during sex the way he dictates. We may have to either act as if we are enjoying it or we will be accused of being frigid. Alternatively we may not be allowed to act as if we are enjoying is as we will be accused of being a 'slag'.

He uses violence
The Sexual Controller rapes us. He also rapes us when we are asleep. I have heard this so often from women on the programme that we have now coined a new phrase, 'the sleep rapist'! The sleep rapist *only* wants sex when we are asleep. He does not want sex with us when we are awake' i.e. a real person.

He uses our love and desire for him
The Sexual Controller assaults us violently. Then when we are in a heap on the floor he makes tender compassionate affectionate love to us. This achieves several different results. The first is that we confuse the pain of violence with the pleasure of lovemaking. The second is that we are given false hope. We hope that he is now his 'real' self again and that he must love us in spite of everything. So we forgive him and stay with him and drop charges.

If we make advances to him he rejects us. He could call us a 'slag' for initiating sex. He starts to have sex with us then stops abruptly telling us he cannot continue because we are too disgusting. He reluctantly has sex with us and either does not ejaculate or ejaculates prematurely. He then blames us for this.

He will also expect us to remain sexually perfect and insist that we do not breastfeed the baby or give birth naturally. He hurts us by being unfaithful.

The Sexual Controller uses sex to degrade and destroy us
When I first began to use the Freedom Programme for women I assumed that the **Sexual Controller** merely intended to have sex or to 'get his end away'!

However, when I listened to many of the women who came on the programme I began to change my mind.

I listened to dozens of women who said that because they were attending the Freedom Programme they were becoming more confident and starting to challenge their abusive partners. Some were making friends and going to work or college. They all recounted that at that point their abusive partner would become even more sexually abusive.

I then began to realize exactly what **the Sexual Controller** intended to achieve. I began to think about invading armies who rape everyone. They rape old people, men, young babies, *everyone*. I started to see that these conquering soldiers are not raping everyone because they are consumed by lust. They do it to destroy and defeat the enemy. They want to humiliate and crush the enemy and see sexual violation as the most effective way of achieving this. This then is the intention of our **Sexual Controller**.

These are some of the tactics that have been reported to the Freedom Programme over the years. These have come from women survivors who attend the programme, countless health professionals who have completed the training and from the men themselves who have been unnervingly honest. I list them here so that a woman who has experienced this may be able to read this and realize that she is not the only one who has experienced this abuse. She may then begin to understand that she is not responsible.

The Sexual Controller forces us to take part in degrading acts. Rape and buggery has already been mentioned. He forces us to have sex with his friends and with animals.

A practice called 'dogging' receives occasional publicity, especially when a celebrity is involved. Women are taken to car parks or public places and made to have sex in the headlights of other parked cars. This is usually reported in the media as an activity that women consent to or even initiate. However I am now getting information from Refuges and Freedom Programmes across the UK that abused women are being forced to do this.

I have heard two explanations for the term 'dogging'. One is that men who attend such events tell their partners that they are taking the dog for a walk. The other explanation is of course that such men refer to women as 'dogs'.

'Scarfing' is another way of degrading and humiliating women. The abuser puts a plastic bag over his partner's head or strangles her with a scarf. When she begins to lose consciousness he then achieves orgasm and hopefully she can revive. Should the woman die the abuser can then tell the police that this was a mutual sex game that went tragically wrong.

There is apparently a huge 'sex toy' industry on the Internet. Countless perpetrators and survivors have told me that these 'toys' are in fact devices for inflicting sexual torture. A mild example is a 'ball gag'. This is a ball with a scarf attached to it. The ball is put into the woman's mouth and tied in place with the scarf. We than cannot speak and our **Sexual Controller** is having sex with a silent piece of meat. This of course is exactly what he wants.

The Sexual Controller forces us into prostitution. He acts as a pimp. He then assaults us because he says we are 'slags' and uses this as an excuse to members of the legal profession or criminal justice system.

The Sexual Controller demands unrelenting sex all day and night. He will demand it all over the house and interrupt whatever we are doing. This is to make us feel exhausted and dirty. If challenged he would say he has a huge libido or is a sex addict. Several men have contacted me asking if they can come on the programme. They have told me they have problems in their sexual relationships with women. I always respond by asking them if they use sexual abuse in order to degrade and defeat their partners. After a short pause, nearly all of them have answered a straight "Yes."

The Sexual Controller also uses pornography. He makes us watch pornographic films and makes us repeat the actions. He makes us wash with bleach before he will have sex with us. Many women on the programme were also sexually abused as children and subjected to that particular tactic.

The Sexual Controller cuts or breaks stitches after we have given birth. He uses colostomy wounds, which then become repeatedly infected. **The Sexual Controller** is also unfaithful. He has sex with other women. This tactic is a most effective way to degrade and humiliate us.

What does the Sexual Controller believe which allows him to behave in this way?

These are the beliefs that I have heard from the women survivors and the male perpetrators who have attended the Freedom Programme.

The Sexual Controller believes that women were put on this earth to provide sex for men. He also believes that when we are too old for that (usually in our mid twenties) we have no other use. We should then fade out of sight and scrub the house or cook something. He believes that sex is our only value and our only reason to exist. We are not here for companionship or for our value to society.

The Sexual Controller believes we are stupid, helpless pieces of meat who cannot survive without men. He believes that men own us and that we have no right to say "no." to sex with them. He believes that we women do not own our own bodies.

The Sexual Controller believes that all women are 'slags'. He believes that we are 'cannon fodder'. When I heard this I understood it to have two meanings. One is that we are 'expendable troops' in the military sense. The other refers to his penis as the 'cannon'.

When I ask the male perpetrators "does the Sexual Controller like women?" They usually consider this and then reply, "I thought I did, but now I realize my feelings have been more like hatred! " **The Sexual Controller** *does* hate women.

He says that "women are hateful" and "women are toilets." He says that women are for men to empty their 'sack' into and for men to empty their 'dirty water' into. **The Sexual Controller** believes women are not human beings and that we are 'vaginas on legs'.

Where does the Sexual Controller get his beliefs from and how are they reinforced by whichever society he happens to live in?

It would probably be quicker and easier to discuss any ways our society challenges the beliefs of the Sexual Controller!

The beliefs of the **Sexual Controller** have been around for centuries. I understand that women in ancient Greece were isolated, kept in the house and used for breeding and general housework. Ancient Greek men apparently had their meaningful relationships with other men. I have also heard that Aristotle, the father of modern philosophy, is quoted as saying "to embrace a woman is to embrace a bag of manure!" If this is true then that got us off to a very poor start.

One of our most popular English monarchs was Henry VIII. As we may recall he had six wives. He used all the tactics of the **Sexual Controller**, thus providing a role model to reinforce the beliefs of the **Sexual Controller** to this day.

Women have been used as political and economic currency throughout

70

history. The belief that we are property and have no right to say no to sex is expressed by phrases such as, 'lie back and think of England' and 'conjugal rights'.

Various religions give and reinforce the message that we are sexual property and sexual currency. Some Mormons for example have several wives. I recently heard a Roman Catholic Bishop on BBC Radio 4 trying to defend the fact that the church has instructed men with HIV not to wear a condom when having sex with their wives. Women in the groups tell of being advised by priests and vicars that they must give their husbands sex whenever they want it.

Traditional fine art depicts women lying around naked with breasts and genitals on display. Our faces are often in the shadow. In the same exhibitions men are portrayed with factories in the background or standing over a dead animal, which they have killed. They may also be wearing chains of office.

Photographs of naked women are used to promote products such as spark plugs. Half dressed women are used to promote the sale of cars. The vast array of pornography which is available in magazines and on the Internet consistently reinforces the beliefs of the **Sexual Controller**.

Daily newspapers include pictures of women's breasts as a matter of course. Popular music videos and DVDs often have a male singer surrounded by semi naked women who are shaking their breasts. Women singers also appear in various stages of undress.

Clothing for young girl children has also become increasingly sexual. In the last few years a major retail outlet has been heavily criticized for selling thongs for very young girls.

Both men and women on the Freedom Programme have told stories of surgeons who offer to stitch women up "nice and tight!" for him after we have given birth.

I have also heard several anecdotes about surgeons making jokes about the size of women's vaginas when we are anaesthetized for surgery.

Beliefs women share

Women are also bombarded with the same messages as the **Sexual Controller** receives. We believe that we are failures without men and that we cannot survive without men. We believe that our only role is to provide sex for men and that we have no other value.

We believe we have no right to say no to sex and we have no right to initiate sex.

We are constantly told that it is acceptable to see another human being as a sexual object and that other women are competition.

HOW DO ALL THE DIFFERENT ASPECTS OF THE SEXUAL CONTROLLER AFFECT WOMEN?

How are we women affected by being made to have sex against our will?

We can feel owned, powerless and manipulated. We feel as though our only purpose is to provide sex. We lack the confidence to leave the relationship or to stand up to him. This lack of confidence makes it very difficult if not impossible to achieve independence by working. All these effects are very similar to the effects of being sexually abused as a child.

We suffer unwanted pregnancies and we are infected with Sexually Transmitted Infections.

How are women affected by being degraded by sex?

Again these are also the effects of being sexually abused as a child.

We are defeated. **The sexual controller** has used sex as an act of violence, just as soldiers will rape enemies of both sexes, in order to utterly degrade and defeat them.

We feel dirty and degraded and we self harm. We are robbed of our own sexuality. We suffer from eating disorders. We can be driven to drugs or alcohol. We can become promiscuous. I have met some very young women on The Freedom Programme who have so little feeling of self worth that they will have sex for a cigarette or a can of lager. This is the feeling that can drive us to prostitution.

We can also feel afraid, injured, confused, isolated, and unable to trust friends.

How are women affected by having our love and desire for him misused?

If the Sexual Controller rejects us he is in fact telling us that we have no value at all. We have been told by everything we see and hear that our sole reason for existing and our only value is to provide sex. This rejection can therefore be devastating. We also feel like this when he is unfaithful.

If he uses tender lovemaking after violence we can be completely confused and conflate the pain of violence with the pleasure and tenderness of lovemaking. This makes it even more difficult to understand or resist what is happening.

If he tells us that we excite him so much that he ejaculates prematurely we are left with the illusion that we have some measure of control. This too makes it very hard for us to see how much he is controlling us.

How are women affected by living in a society which holds the beliefs of the Sexual Controller?

We have already discussed the magazines, which are aimed at teenage girls. They give a powerful message that a girl's only function is to be an attractive piece of meat. Obviously the only proof that we are an attractive piece of meat will be that we have a boyfriend.

Imagine the scene. We have a young teenage girl. She is doing well at school academically. However, she has no boyfriend and therefore her status is low. She is often being bullied and physically assaulted by the other girls in her class. She meets a boyfriend and everything changes. Other girls in the class start to treat her with more respect. Her status rises dramatically.

The boyfriend starts to demand sex. Our teenage girl is in a dilemma. If she refuses, the boy may well say, "OK! I will go and have sex with your mate!" He does. Our teenage girl is humiliated and her status falls. That is the best scenario. Others are worse.

She may say "OK. I will if you wear a condom." If our young man holds the beliefs of the **Sexual Controller** he may say "It's like having a sweet with the wrapper on!" Our girl may agree. The worst scenario is that she gets pregnant and he tells everyone she is a 'slag' and then has sex with her friend. Her school career is halted and she is humiliated.

Another variation on the result of these beliefs is that teenage girls who believe that to be sexually attractive is their sole function may not try at school.

If we are constantly bombarded with messages about our sexual value and purpose we may see other women as competition. We have affairs with their partners. **The Sexual Controller** could not manage to be unfaithful if we didn't!

We can never be happy with ourselves. We always feel as though we are not living up to the standard of sexual attractiveness we set ourselves. This can lead to eating disorders and plastic surgery.

We measure our own worth by the quality of the man we are with. I can give a personal example of this. Many years ago, when I was young, I had no qualifications and no career. That did not matter to me at the time because I was living with a Barrister! I believed I was successful because I was sufficiently sexually attractive to have a relationship with this man! In other words I measured my own worth by the status of the man I was having sex with!

This was many years ago and my own attitudes have changed

dramatically. However, I still see the same beliefs in women I meet today. Many women go to work in the NHS in the hope of marrying a Doctor! Many young women who come on the programme initially express a longing to become the girlfriend or wife of a footballer!

It is also worth mentioning in passing that we also get a strong message from society that we have no right to say "no" to sex. So instead of saying "no" we make excuses and say we are tired or have a headache.

Let us now go to the opposite of the Sexual Controller. A non abusive man whom I have christened **"The Lover"**.

THE LOVER

How does the Lover behave?

The Lover shows physical affection without expecting it to lead to sex. The women on the Freedom Programme have consistently rated this characteristic of the Lover as their favourite. He also accepts physical affection without it leading to sex. This is the second favourite!

The Lover accepts that his partner can initiate sex and encourages us to do so. If we say no he accepts that no means no and would not expect us to have to make excuses.

The Lover 'makes love' to his partner. He communicates with us during the process and is obviously treating us as a human being. He combines physical affection with sex.

The Lover would expect us both to share decisions about contraception. He is also faithful. He respects our wishes and keeps our confidences. He never talks about his sexual experiences with us to anybody else.

The Lover believes that sex must be freely given and that both participants must be freely informed. There must also be an equal balance of power.

The Lover believes that women are free, equal, and should be independent. He likes us and values us! He has too much respect for women to go to a 'Lap Dancing Club'! He is brave enough to stand up to other men and resist peer pressure to do so.

9

THE KING OF THE CASTLE

*A woman is assaulted on average of 35 times before
she seeks Help.* (Amnesty UK 2006)

THE KING OF THE CASTLE USES
MALE PRIVILEGE TO CONTROL WOMEN

The King of the Castle gets us to do all the menial tasks

The King of the Castle rarely stomps into our life and immediately
starts ordering us to do his housework and cooking. When we first
meet him he may use a more subtle approach. This is how he will
eventually manipulate us until we become an unpaid housekeeper. We
will examine his approach to each individual household task.

Shall we begin with the washing? **Our King of the Castle** will turn up at our house with a little washing for us to do for him. Perhaps a few items of clothing he has left overnight. When we suggest that he is welcome to use our washing machine he will assert that he cannot understand the controls. If we insist, he will then summon us to assist every time he is faced with the task of loading the machine and switching it on.

dirty laundry goes
on the floor.
and eventually
reappears clean
in the cupboard ...
INCREDIBLE

Eventually this may wear us down to the extent that we tell him to leave it for us. However, if we are made of sterner stuff and resist the first stage of the campaign, he has his master plan. He will then add the ubiquitous red sock to the whites. He will very probably play his trump card by washing the whole load at the top temperature. This will ensure the desired result of very small very pink clothes. We are quite likely to admit defeat at this point. Round one is awarded to **the King of the Castle**.

We will now turn our attention to the task of household cleaning. He has a range of tactics to ensure we do this. One of the first is to sit surrounded by a rising mound of detritus. He will create a sea of dirty cups, glasses, plates, ashtrays and newspapers. When we suggest that he cleans up he says, "Just relax, I'll do it later!" Or "Chill!" Or "Stop nagging when I am trying to relax." We soon learn that it is easier to tidy up ourselves than to have permanent confrontation.

Early in the relationship **the King of the Castle** may give in to pressure and plug in the vacuum cleaner. He may miss most of the dirt on the carpets and he is almost certain not to empty the bag. If he dusts inadequately or fails to clean the shower or toilet properly we will eventually succumb and find it easier to do it ourselves.

Shall we now turn our attention to matters culinary? **Our King of the Castle** may cook a meal early on in the relationship. He will almost certainly burn everything. He is also very likely to dirty every utensil in the kitchen and leave it for us to clean up. As with cleaning and washing we are likely to find it quicker and easier to do it ourselves.

The King of the Castle will also complain bitterly if has to do any other task. For example, he may be heard to say, "These dishes are filthy!" He will also describe such tasks as being done for us! He may say "I help her with the housework. I have brought the washing in for you. I have unloaded the dishwasher for you. "

There are a couple of other areas where he needs to establish his rule. In order to ensure we plan the menus and the shopping he will quickly get into the habit of asking, "What's for breakfast? What's for lunch? What's for dinner?" Without being aware of it we will soon begin to answer this and the pattern is set.

In order to ensure that he will never have to put anything away or actually find anything the **King of the Castle** will ask the "Where is?" questions. "Where's my shirt? Where are my socks? Where are the children's clothes?"

Once this primacy has been established **the King of the Castle** can settle into using the rest of the tactics of male privilege.

He will soon feel free to leave his dirty washing on the floor. He can shout when his shirt has not been ironed. He will assume he will get services. He will run his fingers across ledges looking for dust. He will feel free to order us to make cups of tea or to make meals for his friends.

He may start ordering daughters to wait on him and the boys. He will expect his tea on the table at whatever time he walks through the door. He will come and go as he pleases and use the place as a hotel.

He will expect special food and his own chair. He will control all the television viewing by holding all the remote controls. He will leave us impossible lists of tasks to do each day.

The King of the Castle controls all the money. He may keep it all and expect us to ask for every penny we need. He is unlikely to tell us how much he earns. He may also keep his 'pocket money' and expect us to pay for all the household expenses from the rest.

The King of the Castle can also use reverse tactics to control us. He may refuse to let us do anything at all because he says we are so useless we cannot even do housework and cooking properly.

What does the King of the Castle believe which allows him to behave in this way?

When I first started working with perpetrators they told me they believed that women were for CFCs (cooking, fucking and cleaning). That will do for a start.

They also believe that women are so stupid they can be fooled into thinking that men can't look after themselves.

The King of the Castle also believes that the occupation of housework is a second rate and inferior occupation. It is for inferior, second-class citizens.

Therefore, women who are of course inferior beings and second-class citizens should do it.

Housework is therefore beneath men and real men don't do it. Real men however never have to pay anyone to do their housework for them. Real men have women to wait on them without being paid for it.

The King of the Castle believes that only gay men or failures look after themselves. He believes that this behaviour is not abusive but is in fact normal. He also believes that he is the breadwinner because he is a man even when he is unemployed.

Where does the King of the Castle get his beliefs from and how are they reinforced by whichever society he lives in?

The King of the Castle may well have watched his father being **the King of the Castle** and his mother acting as his servant. His mother may have also acted as a servant to him as a boy child. His sisters also may have had to wait on him.

The media reinforces these beliefs by using women to advertise cleaning products. It also sends very insidious messages. Women are depicted as doing housework in most films or plays or soap operas. Women's magazines are dedicated to showing us how to clean and cook. When I was a child I was a Brownie. I was taught how to make beds and set tables.

Everyday words such as 'housewife' provide reinforcement every time it is used. It is especially powerful, as we do not really hear it. Those of us who learned to read using the 'Janet and John' books will recall that Janet and Mummy did all the housework and cooking.

There are many toys, which reinforce the message that women do housework. There are miniature mops and buckets, vacuum cleaners, washing machines and even little sink units!

It may be helpful to place all this in a historical context. During the last World War many men left the UK to fight. As a result women ran the country. We did everything. We ran schools. We drove trucks, flew planes and made bombs. We had excellent wages and we had childcare.

When the men returned from the war the government wanted to give them their jobs back and as a result all the women were dismissed. In order to diffuse discontent the government also used propaganda to persuade women that they didn't want to go out to work, but wanted to stay in the home.

One example of this was the so-called 'Latch Key Kids Study', which was supposed to prove that all delinquent children had mothers who were working.

Having tasted freedom and independence many women were reluctant to go back to doing unpaid domestic work. We needed to be brainwashed into believing that we wanted to be unpaid servants, dedicated only to serving men. We needed to be told that this was our great and glorious destiny.

We also needed to be convinced that we were too stupid to do anything else and that we didn't want to work. We needed to be told that work was very unpleasant and that we were so much better off staying at home and providing domestic support to our husbands.

The 'Good Wives Guide', an extract from 1950's literature was very cleverly designed to achieve these ends. It provides an excellent illustration of this kind of conditioning.

The Good Wives Guide

Have dinner ready. Plan ahead, even the night before, to have a delicious meal ready on time for his return. This is a way of letting him know that you have been thinking about him and are concerned about his needs. Most men are hungry when they come home and the prospect of a good meal (especially his favourite dish) is part of the warm welcome needed.

We are so stupid we need twenty-four hours notice to plan a meal. We need to be told that he likes his favourite food best. Our job description includes being concerned about his needs and the provision of a warm welcome.

Prepare yourself. Take 15 minutes to rest so you'll be refreshed when he arrives. Touch up your make-up, put a ribbon in your hair and be fresh looking. He has just been with a lot of work-weary people. Be a little gay and a little more interesting for him. His boring day may need a lift, and one your duties is to provide it.

There are more details about the job description. We are given instructions concerning our appearance and demeanour. We are also told that work is 'boring' and that it makes people 'weary.'

Clear away the clutter. Make your last trip through the main part of the house just before your husband arrives. Gather up schoolbooks, toys, papers etc. and then run a duster over the tables.

*This is cleverly constructed to remind us how very much **the King of the Castle** is in charge. All activity must now be focussed on his return.*

Over the cooler months of the year, you should prepare and light a fire for him to unwind by. Your husband will feel he has reached a haven of rest and order and it will give you a lift too. After all, catering for his comfort will provide you with immense personal satisfaction.

Our husband is described as needing to 'unwind' after work. Once again we are told that work is unpleasant and therefore not something we would want to do. This paragraph also reminds us how unimportant our needs are. We are not instructed to light the fire to keep the children and ourselves warm, but only when he comes home. We are also considered to be so stupid that we need to be told which season requires the fire to be lit. Remember a few years before this was written we women were manufacturing bombs! We are again reminded that our personal satisfaction must be obtained by seeing to his needs.

Prepare the children. Take a few minutes to wash the children's hands and face (if they are small), comb their hair, and if necessary, change their clothes. They are little treasures and he would like to see them playing their part. Minimise all noise. At the time of his arrival, eliminate all noise of the washer, dryer or vacuum. Try to encourage the children to be quiet.

We are so stupid we need to be told only to wash the children if they are small!

Be happy to see him. Greet him with a warm smile and show sincerity in your desire to please him. Listen to him. You may have a dozen important things to tell him, but the moment of his arrival is not the time. Let him talk first – remember, his topics of conversation are more important than yours.

That puts us firmly in our place!

Make the evening his. Never complain if he comes home late or goes out to dinner, or other places of entertainment without you. Instead, try to understand that his work is strain and pressure, and his very real need is to be at home and relaxed.

Hold it! The sprouts have been cooking for twenty-four hours. We are fresh! We are be-ribboned! The fire is lit and the children have been silenced! The house is gleaming and he is not coming home? Note the reference to work as 'strain and pressure'!

Beliefs we share

Many of us believe that we are naturally responsible for all household tasks. For example, we ask our male partners to 'do us a favour' by unloading the dishwasher or bringing in the washing. I heard a woman recently say that she had asked her partner to clean '**her** windows for **her**'.

When our abusive partners sit and refuse to clean up his mess we do it, we find it very hard to leave it, and so we usually come off worst in this kind of stand off.

We also share the belief that this behaviour is not abusive. I have heard a very successful hard working career woman say that her partner never did housework. He left it all to her but she insisted that he was not abusive.

If we do have a partner who does his share of the housework, our friends tend to praise him as 'marvellous'! We believe that only men have successful careers. Do we also believe that women do not have careers?

How does the King of the Castle affect us?

Many of us are still affected by the blatant cultural conditioning contained in the 'Good Wives Guide' and the advertisements, which are its modern day equivalents.

We see ourselves as second-class citizens and we don't believe we deserve equality or respect. Many of us see it as normal for women to wait on men so we do not challenge his behaviour. Consequently, when the **King of the Castle** comes into our lives his preliminary tactics succeed.

We thank him for doing the dishes 'for us. We believe that we are better at household tasks so it is easy for him to manipulate us into doing them. We believe we can't manage money so we let him take control of it. When he asks, "What's for supper?" and "Where's my socks?" we answer almost automatically.

When he then moves to the second stage of his campaign to use male privilege to control us it is very hard for us to see what he is doing. He then begins to achieve his objectives.

We will then undervalue ourselves even more. We may lack the confidence to meet challenges. We don't go for careers but instead take menial jobs. We don't go to work or college.

We will fall for coercion especially when they say they can't manage without us. We act as doormats. We defer to men at work, socially and in the home and see ourselves as second-class citizens.

If the **King of the Castle** refuses to let us even do any household tasks we then lose the confidence and ability to do anything at all. We become emotionally paralysed.

THE PARTNER

How does the Partner Behave?
The Partner does his share of the housework and does his share of the shopping.

He picks up his own rubbish, and does his share of the ironing.

He cooks food nicely so we can all enjoy it and washes the dishes and pots and pans afterwards.

He uses the washing machine and all the clothes remain the correct colour and size. He uses the vacuum cleaner and remembers to empty the bag.

We have discussions about what we will have for dinner. He knows where everything in the house is kept and never has to ask where things are.

He leaves the remote control on the table and is open about how much he earns.

He never says,

"I *help* her with the housework."

"I have brought the washing in for you."

"I have washed the dishes for you."

"I have cleaned your windows for you."

"I have cooked the dinner for you."

The Partner believes:

Women are equal and we deserve respect.

We are not put on this earth to be an unpaid servant.

The Partner believes that 'real men' can look after themselves.

He is so self-confident that he does not need to have the approval of other men who hold the abusive beliefs of **the King of the Castle**.

10

THE LIAR

Most women are killed or injured when leaving the relationship
(Lees, S. 'Marital rape and marital murder',
In Hanmer, J. et al. Home Truths about Domestic Violence:
Feminist Influences on Policy and Practice: A Reader.
London: Routledge, 2000.)

So far in this book we have discussed many of the tactics used by the Dominator to keep us under control. I have also said that when the Dominator feels that these tactics are failing, he will then use violence.

In this chapter we will discuss the mechanics of an assault

On the next page are the 'Rules of the Game'. Then see the following pages to read my explanation.

RULES OF THE GAME

Women are possessions.
She should obey.

ATTEMPTS TO RE-ESTABLISH THE RULES

Threats, Promises.

ABUSIVE BEHAVIOUR

The tactics of the Dominator keep the rules in place.

VIOLENCE

OK because of the excuses.

SHE REFUSES TO COMPLY

Says 'no', leaves.

EXCUSES

She is a slut,
a bad mother.

BELIEFS ABOUT WOMEN COME UNDER THREAT

Feelings of panic,
powerlessness outrage.

The graphic for the 'Rules of the Game' is a diagram of an assault. I will now take us through this.

The top box is labelled 'Rules of the Game'. These are the beliefs of the **Dominator**. This is how he expects women to behave and also how he expects that he should be allowed to behave. **The Dominator** has hundreds of these 'rules', but I will mention only eight here.

Some of the 'Rules of the Game'.

1. Men own women and women must do exactly as we are told.

2. Women must have no self-confidence. We must never answer back, offer an opinion or make our own decisions.

3. Women should stay at home and not try to have a life of our own.

4. Women should believe and accept all the excuses he gives us for his violence.

5. Women should be responsible for all childcare but expect him to provide discipline.

6. A woman should provide services and act as an unpaid servant.

7. A woman should provide sex on demand.

8. A woman must never be allowed to leave or to end the relationship however violent he has been.

We now look in a clockwise direction to box marked **'Abusive Behaviour'**. Here we have all the tactics, which are used by the **Dominator** to keep his rules in place. I have described the tactics he uses to enforce each rule. I have dealt with them in numerical order.

Abusive Tactics used to keep the 'rules' in place

1. *Men own women and women must do exactly as we are told.* These rules are kept in place by the tactics of The Bully who shouts, glares, sulks, and smashes things.

2. *Women must have no self-confidence. We must never answer back, offer an opinion or make our own decisions.* **The Headworker**, who humiliates us and tells us we are stupid, ugly and useless keeps this rule in place.

3. *Women should stay at home and not try to have a life of our own.* These rules are kept in place by the tactics of **the Jailer.**

The Jailer isolates us by cutting us off from our friends and families. He stops us from working or going to college.

4. *Women should believe and accept all the excuses he gives us for his violence.* These rules are kept in place by the tactics of **the Liar**. He minimises his violence and abuse by using the 'only' word. He may blame drink, drugs or stress. He will never tell us the real reason for his abusive behaviour.

5. *Women should be responsible for all childcare, but expect him to provide discipline.* These rules are kept in place by the tactics of **the Badfather**. **The Badfather** uses children to control us by turning them against us or by threatening to take them away.

6. *A woman should provide services and act as an unpaid servant.* These rules are kept in place by the tactics of the **King of the Castle** who treats us like servants or slaves.

7. *A woman should provide sex on demand.* This rule is kept in place by the tactics of **the Sexual Controller**. **The Sexual Controller** refuses to take no for an answer and forces us to provide sex.

8. *A woman must never be allowed to leave or to end the relationship however violent he has been.* This rule is kept in place by the tactics of **the Persuader. The Persuader** wheedles his way back into the relationship by saying he loves us. He also threatens suicide and violence to ourselves and anyone who has given us help or shelter.

We will now proceed in a clockwise direction around the graphic until we arrive at the next box. This is labelled **'She refuses to comply'**. This deals with **How we break the 'Rules'**.

Before we look in detail at this section it is very important to state that most of the time we do not know what the rules are. The rules also change all the time. One of the rules is that we should always be able to guess what the rules are. Another rule is that we should know when he changes them. It is obvious that we cannot win in this situation.

How we break the Rules

We answer back. We are slow to obey. We look at him. We ignore him. We say no!

We make friends. We get a job. We join a gym. We go to college. We visit our mother. We let a health visitor into the house. We spend too long at the supermarket. We see our friends. We go to the Freedom Programme.

We go to assertiveness classes. We put on weight. We tell him we don't care if we have put on weight. We lose weight. We tell him we saw him hide the keys and his shirt. We tell him we will not take tranquilisers and that we are not mad. We fail to realise that he now takes three sugars in his tea instead of two.

We ask him to leave. We leave. We will not have him back. We report him to the police. We refuse to drop charges. We change the locks. We go to a refuge.

We refuse to believe his excuses. We tell him he is lying and we know exactly why he uses abuse and violence.

We tell him that the children *will* go to bed now and they will eat their dinner. We tell him not to buy those £100.00 trainers for the baby but to pay the money towards the housekeeping instead.

We tell him to make his own tea and to bring us a cup while he is up.

We hold the remote control. We refuse to pick up his dirty clothes from the floor. We ignore the rubbish, which has accumulated round his chosen chair.

We tell him that he *will* take his turn at cooking but this time he will not burn the food. We also refuse to accept that he *cannot* operate the washing machine or dishwasher. If he asks, "What's for dinner?" we say, "How would I know?" If he asks, "Where's my shirt?" we reply, "I have no idea. Why ask *me*?"

We say no to sex. We tell him no means no. We say yes to sex but do not appear to enjoy it. We have an affair. We tell him we are lesbians. We tell him we will not be raped and buggered. We tell him we will not be raped while we are asleep and insist on sleeping in another room. We lock our bedroom door. We take the pill and insist on the use of a condom.

We will now continue to proceed in a clockwise direction around the graphic until we arrive at the next box. This is labelled **'Beliefs about women come under threat'**.

Beliefs about women come under threat

When we break the rules **the Dominator's** whole view of the world is challenged, He tells himself "this should not be happening!" This is as if the dog has answered back! **The Dominator** experiences feelings of panic, powerlessness and outrage. If he does not get those rules back in place he will no longer be a 'real man'! It is important to note that when most women are killed or injured they are leaving a relationship. This session should help us to understand why. *They have broken the rules.*

The Dominator now needs to get the rules back in place. In order to achieve this he knows he needs to use violence. He has a slight problem with the use of violence. If you ask an abusive man if he believes it is acceptable to use violence against a woman he will almost invariably answer, "Only if she deserves it." So in order to assault us he will need to convince himself that we do indeed deserve it. He needs to justify his actions in advance. He needs to 'wind himself up'!

Those of us who have been on the receiving end of male violence know that before he hits us there is always a time when he is not in communication. Women have described it as being as if he is not there. "There is no one home!" During this 'wind up' phase it does not matter what we say because he does not listen. It appears that he cannot hear us or often see us. This is because he is having a dialogue with himself. This could be happening in his head or he could be speaking out loud. He will be giving himself excuses to hit us. These are discussed in the next box which I have labelled **'Excuses for violence'**.

Excuses for violence

He is going to get drunk. This is very common. Often an abuser will drink during the wind-up stage so that he can later blame the violence on alcohol. He will tell himself and others that we drove him to it. He will say things like "I need a drink to live with that bitch!" Men on the programme have told me that they would decide to use violence, go to the pub, drink very little then stagger home and hit their partners. They would later claim to be so drunk they could remember nothing about the incident.

These are some of the other phrases that the men and women on the Freedom Programme have provided over the last nine years:

"She is fucking asking for trouble."

"She is obviously shagging someone else."

"I work my butt off to put food on the table and all she does is sit on her fat arse and eat my food with those slags she calls friends."

"She is pushing my buttons."

"Who wears the frigging trousers in this house?"

 "She knows I hate that!"

"She knows I am suffering from stress!"

"She knows I need sex regularly."

"What sort of a wife is she?"

"She's deliberately winding me up."

"She's asking for it and she's going to get it!"

"How dare she make me feel like this! Who does she think she is?"

"What does she think I am? She needs a good seeing to."

He will also call us abusive and insulting names so that he will see us as less than human. We will then be easier to assault.

"Fucking slag! Fucking cow! Nagging dirty bitch!
Fucking whore!"

Eventually our **Dominator** will be sufficiently wound up to hit us. He does so.

The 'wind up' process can take minutes, hours, days or even weeks. When he hits us we move to the box labelled **'Violence takes place'**. He can live with this because of the way he has justified his actions in advance.

He now needs to **get the 'rules' back in place.** He needs us to comply. He now turns into **the Liar** and uses minimisation, denial and blame. These are the excuses he gives to us or to the police or to probation officers. These are the excuses men bring to the perpetrator programme.

THE LIAR

The Liar uses minimisation

He uses certain words to make it all sound less than it was. "It was *only* a slap. It was *only* a push. It was *just* a joke. We were *only* play fighting. It's six of one and half a dozen of the other. She gives as good as she gets. I *only* hit her when she is drunk."

He lies about what happened

"I had to restrain her because she was hysterical. I thought she was going to hurt herself or the children. She fell and hurt herself. She bruises easily. She was drunk and fell over. I was not using sexual violence. I have a huge libido; I need sex all the time."

"I was defending myself. I am the victim here. Where did she get those bruises? Who did that to her? It certainly was not me. Someone must have broken in and attacked her in the night. We quarrelled."

He lies about why it happened. He blames everything and everyone except himself.

"I was drunk and don't remember a thing. I always have a bad reaction when I drink spirits. I had taken too much heroin or cocaine and it made me aggressive. It always does. I also had a bad reaction to my prescribed medication."

"I suffer from this medical condition which makes me lash out in my sleep. I don't know I am doing it."

"She made me so very angry. She pushed my buttons. She wound me up! I have a short fuse and just lost it! She nagged me until I just lost it! The red mist came down and I was so angry that I blacked out. I just snapped."

"She is mentally ill and it is so difficult to live with her. Now and then I just lash out from sheer frustration."

"The strain of living with a handicapped child finally got to me. The strain of caring for a disabled woman finally got to me. She is such a bad mother that the children suffer because of her. "

"She is the violent one. I am the victim. I need some help. There should be refuges for abused men. Who is going to help me?"

"She is a slag. She made me do it because she was having an affair. She was having an affair and she left me and I was heartbroken. I only did it because I love her. I was out of my mind with jealousy! She deserved it. She had it coming."

"I had a terrible childhood. I suffer from Gulf War Syndrome. I am insecure. I have low self-esteem. My mother abused me. My ex wife was such a bitch and a slag that I find it impossible to trust women."

"I am suffering from anxiety. I am on four different kinds of medication for my stress." "I had a migraine."

95

"I am autistic. I suffer from Attention Deficit Syndrome. I suffer from Tourette's syndrome. I have a borderline personality disorder. I suffer from Othello syndrome (morbid jealousy). I suffer from an Obsessive Compulsive Behaviour Disorder."

"I have been working too hard. I am unemployed. My team lost. I have learning difficulties."

These are only some of the examples of how the Liar uses minimisation, denial and blame to explain away his violence and abuse. The real reason for his violence is that we did something he did not like. He then decided to use violence because he felt that his other controlling tactics were not working. He decided to use violence to increase his control over us.

If we examine the cycle described in Rules of the Game we can see that at no stage is he actually angry. He achieves a state of manufactured outrage but this is not anger. He is fully in control the whole time.

If he wishes to change his behaviour he needs to change his beliefs about women. He needs to change the "Rules of the Game!

How the Liar affects women

We are completely confused. I have heard so many women trying to make sense of their situation by repeating the excuses of the Liar. We do this because his excuses are the only explanation we have and we are trying to explain the inexplicable.

We then have him back or forgive him. We feel trapped and become depressed and anxious. We blame ourselves and believe that we deserve to be abused. Then we try harder to please and placate him, because we believe we caused the violence.

Courts, police, social services or probation officers do not believe us. We even begin to think that we have imagined it.

We start to share the beliefs of the Liar. We may begin to believe that violence is acceptable if we have a good excuse. We may learn to refuse to take responsibility.

We may learn by example to lie, it becomes a habit for us. We can begin to believe that abuse is normal behaviour.

We can believe that the abuse does not affect our children. This can lead to our children being hurt, growing up with distorted beliefs, or being taken into care.

THE TRUTHTELLER

How does the Truthteller behave?

When the **Truthteller** is wrong he admits it. He says things like "I was in the wrong." "That was my fault."

He takes responsibility for his own actions. He never blames other people for his own wrongdoing.

He tells the truth and does so consistently. He is honest with himself and with others. Consequently he can be trusted.

He is a good role model for the children to emulate.

He is honest and accountable in all areas of his life. He is a responsible citizen. He earns his money and pays taxes. He does not claim state benefits to which he is not entitled. He does not take time off work and claim to be ill when he is not.

11
THE PERSUADER

There are 275 refuges for women in England.
(Women's Aid 2004)

HOW DOES THE PERSUADER USE COERCION AND THREATS TO CONTROL US?

How the Persuader uses threats

The Persuader has an enormous arsenal of threats, which he will use to persuade us to have him back or return if we have left him. He will also want us to drop charges.

The Persuader will threaten to kill us, to kill our relatives and friends or to kill the children. The latter is a potent threat because we watch or read the news and we know how many abusive men kill children to take revenge on women who have left them. He may threaten to kidnap the children.

The Persuader may threaten to kill himself. He may attempt suicide or he may self-harm. This can be very effective when done in front of the children. He may then get nurses and doctors or even police to telephone us to say he needs our help.

Many **Persuaders** do kill themselves and then we can suffer for the rest of our lives. Everyone, including the children will blame us. As we are unaware of the tactics of the **Persuader** we too may blame ourselves. We may have years of guilt. **Persuaders** can abuse us from beyond the grave.

The Persuader may threaten to humiliate us. He will threaten to publish intimate photographs on the Internet. This tactic is particularly popular when used against women who have celebrity status. He may threaten to paste such photographs onto walls or lampposts near our place of work.

He may use the courts to threaten us by using the children. He will threaten to sue for custody. He may also threaten to report us to social services. He may say, "If social services know I am supposed to be violent they will take the children." He may have also forced us in the past to have sex in front of the children. He will now threaten to tell social services that we initiated this. The children will not know whose idea it was but they will be able to confirm this happened.

The Persuader may threaten to report us to the DSS for making false claims. He will threaten to claim the house and make us homeless and to become unemployed so he will not have to pay child support. If he is unemployed he can also claim legal aid if he is harassing us through the courts.

The Persuader will threaten to find us wherever we go. He telephones all the time and turns up at all hours. He is particularly fond of using the Badfather tactic of turning up drunk at 2 a.m. He will kick the door down or break windows and demand to see 'his' children.

The Persuader uses coercion, he makes us feel sorry for him.

The Persuader cries. He stands on our doorstep wringing his hands and crying. He says, "What will I do without you?" "Where will I go?" "I love you. I thought you loved me." "It's Christmas! I can't cope without you!" "I've got cancer!"

The Persuader will indicate clearly that he cannot cope without us. He will demonstrate that he is not eating by going on the famous **Persuader diet** and losing two stone in a week. Men on the programme have suggested that this effect is best achieved by wearing clothes that are a couple of sizes too big.

He will also demonstrate that he is not coping by not shaving and looking dirty and unkempt.

The Persuader uses other people to persuade us that he is really sorry. Members of both our families and our friends will form an orderly queue to our door. They will say, "I've never seen anyone so distressed!" "I've never seen anyone love anyone as much as he loves you!" "He's really sorry!" "He's heartbroken!" "He's sleeping on my couch!"

The Persuader uses the children

He tells the children that we are forcing him out and that we want to give them a new daddy. He rents a really horrible flat or caravan. He moves into the garden shed or his car. He then shows the children where we are forcing him to live. He tells us "The children need a father."

He suggests holidays and treats to the children that will only happen if we go along too. He tells the children that he would love to be together as a family at Christmas.

The Persuader makes promises

We will recall some of the excuses the Liar made. **The Persuader** now uses them as the foundation for his promises. He may have used insecurity and low self esteem as excuses. He will now announce that he is seeing a counsellor to help him with these problems.

If he used the excuse that he was drunk **the Persuader** will now arrange to attend Alcoholics Anonymous. He may even suggest that we join the support group!

The Persuader may have identified a gambling addiction as the problem. He will naturally now promise to sign up with Gamblers Anonymous.

If he had used a plethora of medical conditions **the Persuader** is already demonstrating that he is seeking help. He will be able to produce his prescribed medication for his anxiety or stress. He may have blamed an adverse reaction to other prescribed medication and will produce further medical evidence to support this.

The Persuader may have blamed a variety of psychiatric disorders and syndromes. He now promises to visit his GP and ask for a referral to a psychiatrist.

He may have blamed 'anger', "The red mist 'descended' or he may blame his 'short fuse'. This being the case he will undoubtedly now enrol on an 'Anger Management Course'. In the last chapter we identified clearly that he is not angry so this promise is also useless.

The Persuader makes us feel jealous

If all the tactics described above fail, the Persuader has a very powerful card up his sleeve. He will tidy himself up. He will get a job or get a better job. He will move into a nice flat. He may buy a new car. He will also, crucially, get a new female partner!

The Persuader suggests that we help him to change

If we are now starting to weaken or if we have succumbed to the last tactic the Persuader may now make some suggestions as to how we can improve our relationship by changing *our* behaviour.

If he has blamed low self-esteem and insecurity he may ask us to hep him to feel more secure and to raise his self-esteem. This process would be helped if we just agree with everything and never argue.

If we have never been married he may say that this makes him insecure. He will therefore suggest that we do in fact get married.

Perhaps even after we are married he may still tell us he is insecure. He may feel better if we have another baby. He may tell us that our job also makes him feel insecure. He will say he feels very jealous of the men with whom we are working. He will then suggest that we leave work. He will also say this if he has been diagnosed as suffering from 'Morbid Jealousy Syndrome' or 'Othello Syndrome'.

The Persuader may also suggest that the nature of our work damages his self-esteem. He may tell us that he feels less of a man because we have a successful career and he does not. If we were to give up this job he is sure that he would feel much better.

The Persuader may have blamed various medical and psychiatric conditions for his behaviour. He will then tell us that we need to help him recover from these 'ailments'. He will make suggestions as to how we may assist. As he maintains that he is ill rather than abusive it would help if we do not contradict him or distress him.

The Persuader may have blamed us for making us hit him. In order to avoid this happening again he will suggest that it would be better for everyone if we just do as he asks all the time and show him more affection.

The Persuader may have blamed others for his behaviour. He may blame our mother or our sister or our friend for coming between us. He may suggest that we stop seeing these troublemakers. He may blame our child from a previous relationship. He may suggest they go to live with their father. He may also suggest that we move away. His preferred location may be an island in the Outer Hebrides!

What does the Persuader believe which allows him to behave in this way?

The Persuader believes that women have no right to object to violence. We are possessions and should put up with anything he decides to inflict upon us. **The Persuader** believes that if he has a relationship with a woman she automatically becomes his property.

He also believes that 'real men' never allow women to end the relationship. He also believes that 'real men' own us even we don't want them anymore. Women have no right to leave. **The Persuader** believes that if a man allows a woman to end the relationship then that man is not a 'real man'.

The Persuader believes that women are responsible for men's well being. He believes that we should mother men. He also believes that women are responsible for men's behaviour. He does not believe he is responsible for his own behaviour. This belief is closely related to **the Liar's** belief that women make men hit them.

The Persuader also believes that women are so stupid that we will believe anything that he tells us.

Where does the Persuader get his beliefs from and how are they reinforced by society?

The Persuader's belief that 'real men' should never allow women to leave is reinforced every time a man murders a woman and uses the excuse that she was leaving him. He hears this excuse and he then sees the ludicrously lenient sentences, imposed by the Courts.

The beliefs of **the Persuader** are reinforced by every conversation he has with his friends. He and they will tell each other that a 'real man' would never allow a woman to leave him. They will say, like the men in my programme,"A man who finds his wife in bed with another man has every right to kill her!"

The help he receives from friends and family reinforces the beliefs of **the Persuader**. The fact that they will intercede on his behalf supports his belief that we have no right to leave him and that we are responsible for his well-being.

Every professional he meets supports **the Persuader's** belief that he is not responsible for his own actions. He could seek help from the GP who asked his wife "how did you let things get to this stage?"

The Persuader could visit the social worker that blamed women for taking their children into abusive relationships. The same social worker may say that young women get themselves pregnant to impress their friends and get a house. This social worker hates women.

The Persuader may be arrested by the Police Officer who laughed and said, "Did she burn the dinner again mate?" He may then be released on bail by the courts on the same day. The police and the courts may not bother to inform his victim that he has been released.

The Persuader may be harassing his partner for access and may meet the court welfare officer who believes that a violent and abusive man can also be a good father.

The Persuader may visit the counsellor who believes he is violent because he failed to bond with his mother. He may visit a counsellor who believes he is insecure or who colludes with the excuse that he has low self-esteem.

The Persuader may be referred to the psychiatrist who diagnoses him as having a borderline personality disorder. He may also go to the alcohol or drugs worker who believes substance abuse causes violence.

A new girlfriend, who is only too happy to support him against his former partner, will not challenge the beliefs of **the Persuader**.

There are songs such as 'Stand By Your Man', which give a very strong message that women should put up with anything!

Beliefs women share

We obviously do share many of these beliefs, because we do feel responsible for a man's well-being. Many women have said they feel guilty for ending the relationship and sorry for him even if he has been violent. They have identified that we believe we should mother men. We believe we cause the violence.

HOW ARE WE AFFECTED BY THE PERSUADER?

How are we are affected by his threats?

We fear for the safety of our family and friends. We are intimidated so we drop charges and take him back. We are placed in an impossible position. We can either have him back and continue to endure his violence and abuse or we leave him or get an injunction to keep him away. We can then never relax for fear that he will break in and attack us.

Some women have to change their names and move to a different area under the 'witness protection schemes'. This will probably mean they are completely cut off from friends and family and any other support networks. I know several women in this situation who keep in touch with their families and with me using mobile phones or e-mail.

We drop charges. We have him back. Consequently, if our children are on the child protection register because of his violence they may be removed from us and put into care. *A woman is murdered every three days.*

How are we affected by his use of coercion to make us feel sorry for him?

This tactic is very effective. It is hard to see the situation clearly when we are being subjected to such Oscar winning performances. It is especially difficult when the supporting cast of family and friends join in.

As a result we believe him when he says he is broken-hearted and has cancer.

Many women have said they feel guilty for ending the relationship and sorry for him even if he has been violent. When we do have him back friends, relatives, and other agencies give up on us and then we become even more isolated.

How are we affected by his use of the children?

We are hounded through the Family Courts. If we are working and he is claiming legal aid we cannot afford legal fees. Some men actually represent themselves in court and use the Family Court setting to continue to intimidate us.

The Persuader has turned the children against us using the tactics of the **Badfather**. He has also kept at least one child with him all the time. As a consequence we cannot leave with the children. I have met several women who have been forced, out of fear for their own lives, to abandon the children and flee without them.

How are we affected by his promises?

We are very likely to believe the excuses he gives for his violence and abuse. Why should we not believe them? Everybody else does! We have been given no other information unless we attend the Freedom Programme or read this book.

If we believe his excuses we are likely to believe his promises. We believe that of course he must have been drunk when he hit us. It is obvious. He was staggering around and smelled of beer. So we have faith in his promise to get help with his drinking.

We then have him back and the men on the programme tell me that after a very short time they revert to their former level of abuse or raise it because they feel even more confident that they will get away with it. We then feel confused and helpless.

How are we affected when he makes us feel jealous?

We may think that as we have put up with his former bad behaviour for years that we deserve to share these improvements. We will not want our successor to reap the benefits now. This tactic may well succeed where all the others failed! We may have him back. This can be a big mistake as **the Persuader** may decide to keep his new partner and therefore become 'King of Two Castles'!

How are we affected by his suggestion that we help him to change?

We accept his suggestions for improving our relationship. We may then stop work and become more isolated and more financially dependent. We may stop seeing our friends or family and become even more isolated.

We may agree to have another baby so we will be tied to the house again for another four years. While we are pregnant he has more opportunity to emotionally abuse us by telling us we are fat and ugly.

We may agree to marry him. This will give him even more legal control over us and make it even more difficult to separate from him in the future. We may also move to the Outer Hebrides with him!

We may give in to him more and become generally more compliant because we believe he has trouble managing his 'anger'. We are more likely to give him sex whenever he wants it. We may become even more diligent in our execution of household tasks.

If the tactics of the Persuader succeed, the overall effect is that he achieves a greater level of control than he had before we tried to leave.

THE NEGOTIATOR

How does the Negotiator behave?

The Negotiator takes responsibility for his own well-being. He also takes responsibility for his own behaviour.

He accepts that another person has a right to end the relationship with him.

He will then be able to negotiate how we can do this with as little distress and damage to either party.

He will wish to negotiate how the separation can be managed with minimum damage to the children.

He regards women as free, independent and equal. He does not believe it is possible to own another human being. He accepts that women have a right to leave men if they wish to.

He is interested in our well-being and can admit to being wrong.

12
RESOURCES

*In the UK a woman is assaulted in
her home every six seconds.*
(Professor Stanko, E. 'The Day to Count:
A Snapshot of the Impact of Domestic Violence in the UK'.
Criminal Justice 1:2, 2000.)

WHAT RESOURCES ARE AVAILABLE
TO WOMEN WHO ARE BEING ABUSED?

The Domestic Violence Police
These specialist units should now be in place all over Britain.
Typically, uniformed police respond to 999 calls. Whether or not
a perpetrator is arrested and charged, they will pass the information
about the call to the specialist Domestic Violence Police. Officers
from these units will usually make some kind of follow up contact
to offer women some support.

Many women on the programme have had bad experiences with
police in the past. In recent years, particularly with the introduction
of the Domestic Violence Police, the situation has greatly improved.
Nevertheless, as in any large organisation, there are still some areas
where there is room for improvement.

Women's Aid
They provide refuges, which are valuable resources for women who
seek shelter for themselves and their children. Some women express
a fear that there is some stigma involved in going to a refuge, but
there have been many others in the group who will have found the
experience positive. Many women say that going to a refuge saved
their lives.

Many refuges also offer outreach support for women who have
elected to remain in their own homes. Many refuges and Women's
Aid organisations across the UK provide the Freedom Programme
as part of their service to women. Their contact numbers are also

included in the list of Freedom Programme providers on my web site (www.freedomprogramme.co.uk).

Information about available help is now posted in libraries, doctors' surgeries and hospitals. Help line numbers are frequently posted on the sides of buses. There are Notional Domestic Violence Help Lines in England and Wales. Internet search engines are very helpful.

13
WARNING SIGNS

This chapter is influenced by some work I did with the male perpetrators from the original probation programme in 1996. In that session I asked the men to write a letter to a real or imaginary daughter. In the letter they warned her which behaviours to look out for in a new boyfriend.

Later, the women on the Freedom Programme started to compare notes during the sessions. Many said that they had left their abusive partners and then met a new one. The new one was completely different from the old one so they assumed that he was not an abuser. Wrong! He was just as abusive but in a different way.

So in this session we try to guess how a **Dominator** would show himself in the first two weeks of the relationship. Here are some of the many warning signs provided by hundreds of men and women from the Freedom Programme over the last nine years.

WARNING SIGNS OR 'HOW TO SPOT A DOMINATOR'

Early Bully
He may go quiet for a short time. This could be a 'sulklet', he will not explain why. He may stare or glare or have our **'Bully'** smile, which means he is smiling with his mouth and glaring with his eyes.

He may be aggressive with others. Perhaps he may bully bar staff or waiters. He may use all the body language of **the Bully**. Watch out for tapping fingers, folded arms and swinging feet.

If we express an opinion with which he disagrees he will not let it go. He will railroad us until we agree with him. He may assume the crotch-thrusting position.

He may tell us very early in the relationship that he would never hit a woman. *Why would he need to say this at all?*

Early Jailer
Many of these tactics are very hard to recognise unless you have done the programme or read the book. Many of us would see them as romantic or loving. Films and fairy stories tell us that these tactics are

the face of true romance.

We want to visit a friend and he insists on dropping us off and collecting us. He *may* genuinely be trying to protect us from the elements or he *may* be making sure we are where we say we will be and there are no men there.

He comes on too strong, wanting to see us every day. He buys us a mobile phone to 'make sure we are safe'. He telephones and sends texts all the time. When he calls he asks where we have been and who with.

He calls round late at night unannounced. He does not want to socialise with our friends. He may try to sow seeds of doubt in our minds about our friends. For example he may ask, "How well do you know Sharon?" "Why do you ask?" We may say? "No particular reason." he may reply. This will leave us with an uneasy feeling about Sharon. He has implied that he knows something we do not.

He will tell us that we do not need to work. He tries to persuade us not to go to work by suggesting we have the odd day off to be with him. He uses phrases like 'together for life' and 'always'.

He tries to monopolise our time. He makes exhaustive plans, which involve being with him all the time. If we tell him that we usually go out with our friends on Thursday nights he will 'forget' this and arrive with surprise tickets for an expensive show or film. We then do not want to disappoint him so we miss our night with our friends.

Early Headworker

He will tell racist, sexist or homophobic jokes. He does not use our name. He calls us 'love' or 'babe' or 'princess' or refers to us as his 'bird'. He puts us down in front of others but always uses humour to do it. He makes sexist remarks about women generally. He will criticise other women in front of us. He will also praise their looks or figures to us.

He stands us up or arrives late. He will be generally patronising and may begin to play mind games in the first two weeks. We feel uneasy but ignore it.

He may make insulting comments about our appearance under the guise of a compliment. For example "You would be really attractive if you were slimmer!"

Early Persuader

He will try to make us feel sorry for him. He may combine this with the **Jailer** tactic of buying the surprise tickets. He will try to persuade us to do something we do not want to do. An example of this could be to persuade us to eat or drink something we do not want.

Early Liar

This Liar may tell us he has a failed relationship. He will have a sob story about a horrible woman who took all his money and now will not let him see his children. He will not use her name. He may call her 'the ex'! He will accept no responsibility for any of this and will blame his former partner for giving him a bad time.

He may tell us he is insecure and has low self-esteem. He may tell us he is the victim of domestic violence.

Early Badfather

As we have mentioned **our Badfather** will probably not have contact with his own children. However he will start to try to use our children to control us. He may very quickly make himself indispensable. He will provide financial support, practical help and treats for the children.

This is very hard to resist if we have been struggling to manage time and finances on our own. Once established he may subtly begin to dispense discipline. He may ask, "Do they always stay up so late?" He may say, "You should not let them speak to you like that!"

Early King of the Castle

He will begin to choose our clothes in very subtle ways. "You look lovely in that dress, but have you ever thought of wearing blue?" He moves in with us too soon. He often achieves this by leaving things at our house.

In **the King of the Castle** chapter we have identified how he gradually manipulates us into doing all the household tasks. **The King of the Castle** also controls all of our lives and takes over our house. He may offer to do everything for us initially and it is but a short step from there to not allowing us to do anything.

For example, if we go shopping for groceries and we select a loaf he may take it out of the trolley and replace it with another. If we vacuum the carpet or wash the dishes he may do these jobs again claiming that we have not done them properly.

The DIY Merchant. He starts doing our DIY as soon as he meets us. He will call round and say, ''I'll be round tomorrow with my tool box to fix those shelves." Before we know it Dado rails have sprung up all over the house! He can then come round and rip them down if we try to end the relationship.

Early Sexual Controller

He may move too quickly and want us to do things, which make us uncomfortable.

He is not actually communicating with us if we do have sex with him.

He is irresponsible about contraception. He refuses to wear a condom. He is married or in another relationship. He may grope us in public.

These warning signs will come in clusters. They will not just exhibit one sign but will display several at a time. We will have noticed more than we realise. We then feel uneasy but ignore it. Women on the programme say that when they have done this session they now take those feelings of unease very seriously.

So, if our new partner exhibits clusters of such tactics it may be time to recall our Fairy Story and say to ourselves, "I don't fucking think so!"

never give up